Moral Matters

A Philosophy of Homecoming

Moral Matters

A Philosophy of Homecoming

Mark Dooley

Bloomsbury Academic
An imprint of Bloomsbury Publishing Plc

B L O O M S B U R Y
LONDON • NEW DELHI • NEW YORK • SYDNEY

Bloomsbury Academic
An imprint of Bloomsbury Publishing Plc

50 Bedford Square
London
WC1B 3DP
UK

1385 Broadway
New York
NY 10018
USA

www.bloomsbury.com

**BLOOMSBURY and the Diana logo are registered trademarks
of Bloomsbury Publishing Plc**

First published 2015

British Library Cataloguing-in-Publication Data
A catalogue record for this book is available from the British Library.

ISBN: HB: 978-1-47252-615-1
ePDF: 978-1-47252-786-8
ePub: 978-1-47252-340-2

Library of Congress Cataloging-in-Publication Data
A catalog record for this book is available from the Library of Congress.

Typeset by Deanta Global Publishing Services, Chennai, India

For Peter

Contents

Introduction

From loss to love

This is a book about home, memory and identity. At a time when people are rapidly disengaging from those forms of life which once bound them together, it can be argued that our happiness depends on saving and conserving them. We cannot flourish in isolation or by detaching from the social sphere which surrounds us. We cannot truly prosper or progress if we choose to forget where we came from or if we dismiss our inherited moral wisdom. And yet, in opting for loss, separation and homelessness, it seems we have done just that. We have opted for a rootless existence where alienation and amnesia are the norm. As I suggest in Chapter 1, while it is true that we have never been more connected, it is equally true that we have never been more disconnected. In constantly communicating through screens and gadgets, we have rejected reality for virtual 'reality'. In so doing, we have fundamentally transformed the way in which we relate to each other and the world. We have forgotten what it means to belong to a place, community, country, culture and church. In effect, we have become exiles to ourselves and the world around us.

One of my central contentions throughout this work is that this culture of alienation and amnesia has its foundations in *liberalism*. As defined by Roger Scruton, liberalism 'conveys the political sentiments of the modern person, who sees himself as detached from tradition, custom, religion and prejudice, and deposited in the world with no guidance beyond that which his own reason can provide'.[1] It is a philosophy of freedom from all inherited obligations and attachments, one that prioritises the individual and his rights over the claims which the wider world makes upon him. As I use it here, however, liberalism refers to all those modern movements which seek to 'liberate' people from what Jean-Jacques Rousseau dismissively called their 'chains'.[2] In this loose sense, it refers as much to the theories of classical liberals such as John Stuart Mill as it does to those of postmodern philosophers such as Friedrich Nietzsche, Michel Foucault and Jacques Derrida. Despite their ostensible differences, what unites these thinkers is a common desire to cast off the chains of custom and to see, as Richard Rorty put it, 'everything wonderfully, utterly changed'.

As it happens, I spent part of my life as a liberal. I grew up in Ireland at a time when the influence of the Catholic Church was pervasive. I was educated by the religious orders, served Mass and shared my family's conservative convictions. However, when the Irish Church experienced its first major crisis in the early 1990s, I embraced many of the theories I critique in this book.

My first major publication was *The Politics of Exodus*,[3] a book on the nineteenth-century Danish philosopher Søren Kierkegaard. I argued that this great thinker of the 'single individual' should be read as a postmodernist before his time, someone who challenged the 'established order' in the name of those who are different, alien and other. In fact, I went further and suggested that he be regarded as the true father of 'deconstruction', the fashionable movement made popular by French intellectual Jacques Derrida. Both Kierkegaard and Derrida sought to undermine the 'system' of G. W. F. Hegel, the philosopher who first perceived what we stand to lose when we make a virtue of estrangement.

For Hegel, self-understanding involves recollecting and identifying with one's past, one's culture, one's religion and the soil itself. It involves retaining and preserving those things which enable us to surmount alienation and to find a home here on earth. It was Hegel's philosophy of homecoming, his belief that self-knowledge involves domestication of those things which initially appear strange and alien, that made him the principal target of thinkers like Kierkegaard and Derrida. If Hegel specified conservation and identity, his opponents emphasised loss and difference. And even though Hegel was my first great philosophical passion, I considered it an ethical duty to side with his opponents. In the decade that followed, I wrote extensively on Derrida,[4] American deconstructionist John D. Caputo[5] and pragmatist Richard Rorty.[6] I owe to each of these great writers an immense debt of gratitude for their personal guidance, wisdom and friendship. However, I could not escape the lingering thought that Hegel was right, that his vision of the human condition was more in touch with reality than that proposed by his detractors.

This belief was reinforced when, in 2002, I began writing a political column for the *Sunday Independent*.[7] I quickly discovered that the problems of contemporary society stem, in large part, from a rejection of the family, the home, tradition, established borders and cultural and religious identity – those things, in short, which Hegel saw as the key to self-fulfilment but which are routinely undermined by his liberal and postmodern heirs. Writing as a journalist enabled me to see that what we have inherited is something precious and, unless we actively strive to conserve it, there is no guarantee that it will last. When, for example, I wrote in support of a group of Irish Muslims seeking to restrain extremist elements within their community, I was threatened by those elements. This proved to me that the greatest risk to our way of life is posed by what my fellow countryman Edmund Burke aptly called 'an armed doctrine'. He was, of course, referring to the revolutionary Jacobins who were then laying waste to France under the banner of 'liberty, equality, fraternity'. As I see it, however, Jacobinism is as much a feature of the contemporary world as it was in 1789.

In defining Jacobinism, Burke wrote that it is 'the attempt … to eradicate prejudice out of the minds of men, for the purpose of putting all power and authority into the hands of persons capable of occasionally enlightening the minds of the people. For this purpose the Jacobins have resolved to destroy the whole frame and fabric of the old societies of the world, and to regenerate them after their fashion.'[8] The new Jacobins may, as in the case of radical Islamists, seek to overthrow Western civilisation by violent means. More common, however, are those who 'form themselves into associations for the purpose of destroying the pre-existing laws and institutions of their country' and who seek to undermine 'by judgments, or otherwise, those who make any struggle for their old legal government, and their legal, hereditary, or acquired possessions'.[9] Burke called this 'Jacobinism by establishment', and it is this which I have come to see as the greatest danger to our shared form of existence. That is because I am convinced, as stated by Michael Sandel, that 'intolerance flourishes most where forms of life are dislocated, roots unsettled, traditions undone. In our day, the totalitarian impulse has sprung less from the convictions of confidently situated selves than from the confusions of atomised, dislocated, frustrated selves, at sea in a world where common meanings have lost their force'.[10]

Few contemporary thinkers share that view, but one in particular has seen with stunning conviction how all faith is cast in doubt, all morality relativised 'and all simple contentment destroyed, by the sarcastic criticism of those who could see just so far as to question the foundations of social order, but not so far as to uphold them'.[11] That thinker is the English philosopher Roger Scruton, and it was he who provided me with my way back home.[12] Scruton convinced me that there is nothing worthy in change solely for its own sake. He taught me the truth of what Hegel and Burke had long ago recognised, which is that we will not look forward if we do not first look back. He proved to me that culture is that which knits society together, and it is, therefore, a 'sacred task' to conserve it.[13] In deconstructing it, we lose that vital wisdom upon which our fragile cultural, political and religious ecology depends. It is to put alienation in the place of affection and licence in the place of loyalty. Through Scruton, I also rediscovered the beauty, truth and consolation of my old religion, a comprehensive defence of which I mount in my most recent work *Why Be a Catholic?*[14]

The present book constitutes my attempt to show why, in all its multifarious forms, liberalism leaves us isolated and alone. As I will say at various stages, *we long to belong*. Deep down, we yearn to be affirmed, recognised and endorsed as part of something more than a loose collection of liberated individuals. If this is a conclusion I have reached at the end of a long intellectual journey, it is something I have also experienced personally as a parent. Since moving to the *Irish Daily Mail* in 2006, much of my journalism has been devoted to my life as a father endeavouring to raise three children in the internet age. As I said at the outset, this is a world robbed of its certainties, one in which displacement and estrangement have become the norm. People 'plug in' so as to avoid the effort of human interaction. They play sport on the Wii, thus sparing the time and energy of having to do the real thing. They make friends on Facebook, thus bypassing the complex process of really having to *make* friends. The moral price we must pay for this is obvious: we have so many 'friends', and yet we have never been lonelier. We are in constant communication, and yet we have lost the capacity to converse. We tweet and text our way through the day, and yet, compared to previous generations, ours is illiterate. In so many ways, our gadgets and toys add to the confusions, as Sandel sees them, 'of atomised, dislocated, frustrated selves'. They are the perfect playthings for those 'at sea in a world where common meanings have lost their force'. This is a world of fake friendship, a loveless and impersonal domain where cheap substitutes diminish all that is beautiful in the human condition.

It could be argued that Derrida signalled the dawn of the cyber age when he famously announced the 'end of the Book and the beginning of writing'.[15] In Derrida's sense, writing signals loss, detachment and even death. If authors are not fully present in their texts, it is because all writing is comprised of marks and traces which cannot completely contain the meaning or intention of the writer. In print, the original meaning is lost as the text detaches from its author and is disseminated to multiple readers. As only a trace of the author remains in his writings, readers must interpret what they think the author is seeking to convey. In emphasising the absence or 'death' of the author, Derrida anticipated the 'textual' age in which writing no longer roots or binds. To tweet and text is not to sit before a blank page and slowly fill it with feeling, emotion and love. Essentially, it is nothing more than a minimalist transmission of electronic data. It is a message drained of human blood.

If, as I believe, we are now living in a world without feeling, it is because we have become a species that seeks sanctuary behind a screen. In so doing, we avoid the effort that real human relations require. We avoid having to expose the true self by refusing to commit ourselves on paper or in person. I want to counter this by arguing that when writing ceases to convey a tangible sense of someone speaking from somewhere, we will lose memory, meaning and all those things which redeem humanity from estrangement. I want to say that behind every gadget and screen, there is a real being, one that cannot be reduced to a cyber pseudonym. I want to make a case for genuine writing and communication, as that which contains the consciousness of the human person in all its aspects.

While letters may fail to completely capture their authors' intentions, it is no less true that each line and curve, dot and cross reveals something about the absent person. They bring before the mind's eye a thousand lost memories. You are reminded of the author's smile, scent and even her long silent voice. It is as though the self clings to those little items of correspondence which, unlike a tweet or a text, can last forever. If that is true of a letter, it is equally so in the case of all human traces such as books, buildings, memorials and works of culture. Each connects us to the world of their authors and creators, to those people and places which serve as the basis of our true identity. Even Derrida recognised this, which is why, as he once told me, his worst fear was that his writings would eventually be confined to a tiny corner of cyberspace. Even he hoped that people would always find time to read his work on paper and respond to it in prose.

I believe that if children are not to become alienated from themselves, we must root them to everything that liberal and postmodern society eschews. We must reattach them to all those features of life unknown to the internet generation. We must reattach them to the soil, the family, and their heritage, culture and religion. For that is what it means to be rooted: it means belonging to a place steeped in settlement. It means cherishing the homestead and all who dwell there. It means being bound to those with whom you share a common past and a joint destiny. In this world of noise, I want my children to listen to the sounds of silence. Instead of allowing them to be plugged in, I want them to hear the autumn leaves crunch beneath their feet. I want them to hear the waves lapping against the seashore, the faint breath of a loved one sleeping, the blue tits singing their way into spring. I want them to learn about life and longing through their encounters with real people as distinct from cyber substitutes. In sum, I want them to discover the world as it unfolds before their eyes and not as it is filtered through a screen. Only then will they know what it means to feel secure in a world with no direction home.

All of this is by way of saying that, having returned to my roots, I now see why Hegel was right. That great philosopher of home correctly perceived that alienation is not our natural condition. He saw more clearly than any of those who followed him why it is folly to deny, destroy or deconstruct those things which enable us to conquer estrangement. He saw the madness in choosing a life of isolation and detachment over one that binds us to time, place and people, thus providing our pathways home. If this sounds like nostalgia, that is because in a fundamental sense, it is. Deriving from the Greek *nostos*, nostalgia means 'homecoming'. Hence, to be nostalgic means to opt for belonging over exile, for attachment over estrangement, for love over loss. My hope is that what I say here will convince you why love will always be preferable to loss and why our survival depends on knowing the difference between the two.

This book seeks to distil the central message of my weekly column in the *Irish Daily Mail*.[16] Entitled 'Moral Matters', it aims to provide readers with a brief moment to take stock of what we take for granted and so often appreciate only when it is too late. I should like to thank all my editors at the *Daily Mail* for giving me the space to develop the themes which form the basis of this work. In particular, I wish to acknowledge Sebastian Hamilton, Ros Dee and Eric Bailey for their constant support, friendship and guidance over many years. In a very special way, I would like to thank my *Irish Daily Mail* readers for their loyalty and devotion to my column. They have convinced me that most people do not want to live in a world without meaning or morality. I hope this work will convince them that there are concrete ways to resist this 'age of normal nihilism', ways which may not turn back the tide but which will make it much easier to swim against it. I am profoundly thankful to my commissioning editor at Bloomsbury, Liza Thompson, for her vision, encouragement and patience. I am eternally grateful to my friend Alexandra Slaby for reading previous versions of this work and for suggesting how it might be improved. In so many ways, she has saved me from myself. Above all, I wish to thank my wife Laura and our dear children, David, Matthew and Peter, without whom I would still be lost.

Notes

1   Roger Scruton, *Dictionary of Political Thought* (Hampshire: Palgrave
    Macmillan, 2007), p. 395.

2   I refer to Rousseau's famous opening line of *The Social Contract*:
    'Man was born free, and he is everywhere in chains'. Jean-Jacques
    Rousseau, *The Social Contract* (Harmondsworth: Penguin, 1972), p. 49.

3   Mark Dooley, *The Politics of Exodus: Søren Kierkegaard's Ethics of
    Responsibility* (New York: Fordham, 2001).

4   Mark Dooley and Liam Kavanagh, *The Philosophy of Derrida*
    (London: Acumen, 2007).

5   Mark Dooley (ed.), *A Passion for The Impossible: John D. Caputo in
    Focus* (New York: SUNY Press, 2003).

6   See Mark Dooley, 'In Praise of Prophesy', in Mark Dooley (ed.),
    A Passion for The Impossible, pp. 201–28.

7   I wrote a column on foreign affairs for the *Sunday Independent* before
    moving to the *Irish Daily Mail* as a cultural and political columnist
    in 2006.

8   Edmund Burke, 'Letter to William Smith (January 1795), cited in
    Russell Kirk, *Edmund Burke: A Genius Reconsidered* (Wilmington:
    Intercollegiate Studies Institute, 1997), pp. 201–2.

9   Edmund Burke, 'Letter to William Smith (January 1795), cited in
    Russell Kirk, *Edmund Burke*, p. 204.

10 Michael Sandel (ed.), *Liberalism and its Critics* (New York: New York
    University Press, 1987), p. 7.

11 Scruton, *Philosophy: Principles and Problems* (London: Continuum,
    1996), p. 14.

12 See Mark Dooley, *Roger Scruton: The Philosopher on Dover Beach*
    (London: Bloomsbury-Continuum, 2009), and Mark Dooley (ed.)
    The Roger Scruton Reader (London: Bloomsbury-Continuum, 2001).

13　See Scruton, *The Philosopher on Dover Beach* (Manchester: Carcanet, 1990), p. 106.

14　Mark Dooley, *Why Be a Catholic?* (London: Bloomsbury-Continuum, 2011).

15　Derrida, *Of Grammatology*, trans. Gayatri Chakravorty Spivak (Baltimore: The Johns Hopkins University Press, 1976), pp. 6–26. I shall expand on this theme in Chapters 8 and 9.

16　A collection of these columns is available at www.drmarkdooley.com.

1

Homesickness

On the surface, we have never been more connected. We are plugged in to a global network powered by a constant craving to communicate. Electronic engagement has made it possible to defy natural boundaries in a way inconceivable to our forebears. Traditional allegiances and loyalties no longer matter to a generation that belongs to a nowhere which is everywhere. Family, home, society and State are meaningless concepts to people divided solely by a power switch. In such a world, individuals are not defined by language, religion or place. Identities are established on Facebook and across chat rooms, virtual congregations where countless communicants are bound by a common host.

In many ways, the information age is a spirit-world where we trade in the immaterial. Relationships are formed and information is shared with people we almost never meet. We call this 'social networking', and yet it bears little resemblance to what we once termed 'social life'. To have a social life meant leaving the isolation or privacy of one's own space to be with others in a public context. It meant interacting with others in communion and conversation. It meant taking time to share a meal, to celebrate, worship or mourn. It involved making lifelong friends.

Virtual reality has radically transformed our concepts of space, time and being with others. We constantly communicate and 'chat' without ever really speaking. We belong to countless chat rooms and social media sites, yet we don't really belong anywhere. When we communicate, it is through instant messaging. The very idea of 'taking time', or of moving beyond the moment, is alien in such a domain. It is a culture of immediacy in which only the present moment matters. There is no past or future in cyberspace, only a perpetual 'now' in which all desires must be instantaneously gratified. It is a no man's land devoid of the public–private distinction, a spectral sphere where no one can hide, a domain where no one ever sleeps. I call it *Cyberia*.[1]

We are fully charged and connected, and yet, at another level, we have never been so detached or disconnected. Isolated, we sit before screens and gadgets divorced from the real world and from real people. Th e great paradox is that by seeking to connect socially, we become evermore solipsistic and secluded.[2] We become evermore alienated and estranged from reality, from human beings and their moral and emotional requirements. We become strangers to ourselves, to others and to the world. To put it simply, the so-called 'information age' has altered the very concept of human identity beyond recognition. We exist in the world, and yet we do not fully belong to it. We are wired to an ephemeral space, having severed our roots from the real. Homelessness is the condition of those exiled to Cyberia.

Cyberia brings to fruition all those secular and liberal ideologies dedicated to emancipating humanity from its natural, historical and cultural constraints. The individual is 'liberated', not only from the chains of custom and tradition but also from truth, meaning and reality. He 'belongs' to a domain of iridescent images, a spectral sphere where people are never present to themselves. In this borderless world, we do not depend on others for self-endorsement or affirmation. We create our own identities, projecting our preferred self-images onto the screen. Local attachments in real space are rejected in favour of a universalism devoid of hierarchy, distinction and ethnicity. It is an egalitarian utopia in which no one is denied a voice and where every opinion is freely expressed without concern for the consequences. It is, moreover, a pleasure paradise which facilitates any and all 'experiments in living'[3] irrespective of the moral repercussions for those still rooted to the real.

What does it mean to 'make' a friend? In Cyberia, it is as easy as clicking on a mouse and involves no effort. In real life, it requires risk, commitment, energy and sacrifice. As Aristotle put it, 'friendship seems to consist more in giving than in receiving affection'.[4] It involves surrendering the self for the good of the other. It requires negotiation, compromise and consideration, all of which are absent from Cyberia where there is little in the way of consolation, community or company. This raises the questions, What personal cost is there when you are shielded from another by a screen? Who cares if you lose a friend on

Facebook when a dozen more can be generated in an instant? The bother of having to actually make a friend, or to commit to something real, enduring or lasting, is short-circuited by a process which does not even require getting out of bed. That is why those enslaved to Cyberia inevitably succumb to loneliness and boredom. For, it is a simple truth that human beings cannot thrive where genuine interaction does not exist.

In the early nineteenth century, a Danish philosopher, Søren Kierkegaard, wrote a pamphlet identifying what he perceived as the 'plague of the age'. For Kierkegaard, that plague was 'a monstrous abstraction, an all-encompassing something that is nothing, a mirage – and this phantom is *the public*'. The public, for Kierkegaard, was not comprised of existing individuals but an abstraction which levels all real distinctions between people. If the public 'creates no situation and no community', it is because it is 'made up of unsubstantial individuals who are never united or never can be united in the simultaneity of any situation or organisation, and yet are claimed to be a whole'. It is a 'corps, outnumbering all the people together', but one that 'can never be called up for inspection'. In a remarkable passage which anticipates the dawn of Cyberia, Kierkegaard writes:

> The public is not a people, not a generation, not one's age, not a congregation, not an association, not some particular persons, for all these are what they are only by being concretions. Yet, not a single one of these who belong to a public is essentially engaged in any way. For a few hours of the day he perhaps is part of the public, that is, during the hours when he is a

nobody, because during the hours in which he is the specific person he is, he does not belong to the public. Composed of someones such as these, of individuals in the moments when they are nobodies, the public is a kind of colossal something, an abstract void and vacuum that is all and nothing ... the most dangerous of all powers and the most meaningless.[5]

Prophetically, Kierkegaard foresaw the disturbingly negative consequences of 'chattering', which he defined as 'an abstract noise that will render human speech superfluous, just as machines make workers superfluous'.[6] When individuals are swallowed up by such an all-encompassing system, the 'coiled springs of life-relationships' lose their resilience. People speak without speaking and exist without truly existing. What emerges is 'an age without passion', one with 'no assets of feeling in the erotic, no assets of enthusiasm and inwardness in politics and religion, no assets in domesticity, piety, and appreciation in daily life and social life'.[7] It is an age of opinion and information, and yet one without essential knowledge and truth. Put simply, Kierkegaard anticipated the 'death of man' in Cyberia. He recognised that belonging to a spectral sphere numbs people to reality, anaesthetises them to 'life's existential tasks'. We become alienated from the concrete structures which once enabled us to negotiate with the environment and with others. Estranged and detached from the social and moral demands of the real, the individual no longer recognises this world as 'home'. He belongs nowhere and to no one, is attached to nothing.

We see this most obviously in our detachment from nature or the land. What was once our natural habitat has become something distant or alien, somewhere we occasionally visit but do not belong. Having been drawn away from the land, we no longer recognise it as our own. We are aliens to the soil, to the earth and to creation. Disconnected and displaced from the material world, we no longer value it as that by which we are sustained and nourished. We no longer value it as that to whose fate we are inextricably bound. In our new world of systems and servers, there is no place for the one system upon which we are ultimately reliant: the ecosystem. Instead of conserving and sustaining its delicate equilibrium, we wilfully contaminate and pollute it. If we do so, it is because it is easy to despoil that with which you do not identify. When you no longer regard somewhere as home, when you no longer perceive it as a source of selfhood, it very soon becomes derelict.

In forgetting how to work the land and husband natural resources, we sever a vital connection to the world and reality. In particular, we lose essential knowledge regarding how to sustain human life at a time of scarce resources. We dispose of that practical wisdom which tells us how to feed ourselves, how to naturally harness heat and light, how to live by the seasons. In forgetting how to adapt to the world, we simultaneously forget how to adapt it to our true needs. We lose sight of the fact that we are corporeal beings with material requirements, whose very survival demands dialectical harmony between the self and its natural environment. Break that essential bond and humanity is not liberated from material bondage. It is exiled and alienated from the only sphere in which it can be truly satisfied. When we cease to rely upon and recognise ourselves as part of nature, when we cease to work on and care for creation, we are evicted from our true home.

The fact that we have already been evicted is dramatically reflected in contemporary living and eating habits. Cyberia, to repeat, is a world of instant gratification, a domain where delays are never permitted and where the fastest always flourish. Ironically, the word 'technology' derives from the Greek *techne*, meaning craftsmanship. The craftsman is someone with particular skills or expertise. He practically engages with the world in order to transform it, and he does so in accordance with the established rules of his trade. The result is a product not only bearing the individual stamp of the craftsman but one formed according to the established wisdom of his profession. *Techne* involves working on the world in the sense of putting a human shape or signature on materials which were formerly alien.

As defined, *techne* bears little resemblance to what we now call 'technology'. If *techne* is a way of practically engaging with reality, technology quite literally cuts us off from it. We relate to the world through phones, gadgets and screens, the result being that we never actually relate to it. Our limbs no longer connect us to the surrounding environment, being as they are mere extensions of electronic devices that fuse us to other devices. Human need and desire are satisfied at the push of a button. What we crave we obtain without having to wait, work or move. We can shop, purchase food, play sport and sometimes even satisfy sexual desire online. We can, in other words, bypass the world and short-circuit all human interaction in pursuit of anything we covet.

To make a home involves domesticating the world. Through design and decoration, we render familiar what was once alien and strange. We shape it in accordance with our self-image. Likewise, in maintaining a garden, we reattach the self to its natural habitat, thus revealing again the secrets of its long-term survival. The family home also provides the setting for communal ceremony, social gathering and rites of passage. In this fashion, family members and their guests celebrate and endorse their common sense of settlement. In sharing a meal, they consume the gifts of the earth, become one with it and, thus, with each other. Through this 'communion', the ties that bind family and friends are sealed. Social endorsement does not exist in a world of fast food and fast living. When we cease to grow, prepare and cook our own food, we are not merely estranged from the earth but from family and society. Fast food is for those without roots, connected only by fibres and wires. It is the perfect diet for citizens or 'netizens' of Cyberia, for those who have repudiated settlement in favour of homelessness and instability.

If the real world is being swept clean of homes, it is because it is now a place of temporary and fleeting attachments. It signals the triumph of immediacy, isolation and individualism. This is not without its civic, social and political consequences. When people are plugged in, they automatically switch off. In our wired world, people still gather socially. They still assemble in cafes and the public square, but even in those contexts, many tend to sit in splendid isolation staring at a screen. Those surrounding them are ignored as they communicate with virtual 'friends' from a virtual community. The most striking consequence of this is that the human face has been erased from the earth like that 'drawn in sand at the edge of the sea'.[8] This means that the social context is no longer a place of casual conversation or chance encounters. Even when packed tightly together on a rush-hour train, we plug in with the aim of zoning out. In so doing, we signal a preference for seclusion and separation over belonging and engagement.

Consider how children, naturally the most social members of our species, are suffering estrangement through technology. Instinctively, all children desire to play. They long to engage with the world so as to make it their own, but they also yearn to connect with others through games and shared interests. Through such imaginative activities, the child develops a sense of self, the environment and, more importantly, social membership. He discovers who he is and where he belongs. However, in the age of Xbox and Wii, these crucial activities are undermined. Instead of imaginatively interacting with others, the child withdraws into a solitary space of his own. Play becomes an isolated endeavour with no connection to anything other than the machine. Even sport, that most physically engaging of all activities, and one which serves as the basis of much social identity, becomes a parody of itself when played online: standing before a screen clutching a remote control, the Xbox generation plays virtual tennis with a cyborg as the sun shines outside. Not only does this alienate them from the natural environment, it also denies them the experience of belonging to something greater than themselves.

Through play, children form friendships and discover the meaning of virtues such as loyalty, courage, responsibility and fairness. Their self-identity is defined and their moral sense is expanded through membership of clubs, teams and camps. They become, in other words, social beings. When, however, their world is mediated through a screen, they cease to engage with others and, thus, cease to truly belong. If this results, as it very often does, in social, learning and behavioural difficulties, it is because we cannot flourish without those forms of membership which only the real world supplies. Virtual or otherwise, we cannot thrive in a vacuum, for we are mutually dependent beings unsuited to isolation and detachment.

It might seem a long way from the playground to politics, but the connection is genuine and convincing. In the absence of real play, there will be no social bonding. When there is no social bonding, people will never acquire that shared sense of belonging upon which the political order depends. To put it another way, when people plug in, they tend to opt out of their social and political obligations. When identities are shaped in the anarchic zone of Cyberia, the political responsibilities of the real world are simply sidestepped. We see this quite clearly in the political apathy characteristic of so many Western nations today. In my own country, the Republic of Ireland, voter turnout rarely exceeds 50 per cent in most polls. If the same is true elsewhere, if political disaffection has become the norm, it is because loyalty to one's fellow citizens, and thus to one's country, is no longer a feature of the modern experience. The 'we' morality which once united communities and societies has withered in the face of rampant individualism. If that is so, it is because when people are only temporarily attached to the real world, they are unable to recognise themselves as integral to it. They are unable to recognise it as home. As a result, they will not see the point of sacrificing for others or for their country. They will demand rights but rarely act from a sense of duty or responsibility.

The basis of genuine citizenship is the experience of membership and belonging. Membership, however, consists of more than merely identifying with a particular place and its current inhabitants. Crucially, it also involves identifying with the dead and the unborn. This was the great insight of Edmund Burke, that defender of true liberty against those who sought to disperse their noble patrimony to 'all the winds of heaven'. In the spirit of Burke, I want to say that connecting with the dead is something communities have traditionally achieved through myths, stories or narratives, and through those cultural, religious and educational institutions whose identity is bound up with that of the deceased. In safeguarding and conserving the 'storehouse of memory', such institutions enable us to converse with the past, thereby making sense of who we are as a people. Without them, we suffer historical and cultural amnesia. We no longer know where our common roots lie, something which naturally results in social and cultural disenchantment. Stated otherwise, when people lose touch with their common past, they cease to understand why they should remain united in the present.

It is no coincidence that there are no dead in Cyberia. There are plenty of ghosts in the machine, but the real dead are without a domicile. This is because there is neither past nor future, only a perpetual present. Living in the instant has, however, its social and moral costs. It means to actively forget the lessons of the past and, therefore, to erase the memory of those to whom the self owes its existence. In connecting with others through devices which detach us from reality, we bypass those institutions which uphold and sustain the historical and moral ecology which supports authentic human life. We cease to recognise ourselves as belonging to anything more fundamental than the chat room or one's personal home page.

Education is an obvious case in point. The primary purpose of education is to impart to children the knowledge which forms the basis of our civilisation. It provides the context in which they learn why we think and act as we do. By engaging with language and literature, mathematics, religion and music, they acquire not only essential information but also an understanding of who they are and where they belong. Through assimilation of the great works of Dante, Shakespeare, Mozart and Dickens, their moral and cultural identity is shaped and nourished. They begin to define themselves in terms of their wisdom and understanding of the world. When observed as such, we see that education is like ecology. That is why reforming the system without due regard to the past is a type of ecological degradation. It also explains why the conventional curriculum was much more than an arbitrary 'aggregate of courses'. It was a sacred covenant binding absent generations, one which formed the basis of intergenerational memory. Without such knowledge, however, we experience a 'homelessness of the mind', for it is this which unites us to the past, thereby supplying a common frame of reference for the living.

In contrast to the knowledge which formed the basis of the traditional curriculum, what we now call 'information' is more akin to functional data. That is, it supplies automatic answers to our immediate inquiries. With one push of a button, the answer to any question or conundrum is instantaneously revealed. Consequently, learning becomes 'processing', rather than a deep emotional engagement with themes and texts, the outcome of which is self-knowledge or identity. When, in other words, education is reduced to PowerPoint presentations, or when, as is the case in my country, subjects such as Shakespeare and history are made optional for students, students are evicted from their intellectual heritage.

If the principal purpose of education is to surmount isolation and estrangement by enabling the student to engage with the past, the information age severs him from it. When the iPad becomes the primary source of a child's knowledge, he enters a space devoid of originality and objectivity. It is a space in which the vital distinctions between knowledge and opinion, truth and falsity are rarely drawn. Hence, the risk is always that the child will never learn how to critically engage with the seminal documents of his tradition, being exclusively immersed in secondary sources. In answering only to his immediate needs, an information-based curriculum thus ensures the student shall never stand 'in the presence of canonised forefathers'. It ensures he shall never be truly at home in this world.

This is not to say that Cyberia is a culture-free zone. Neither is it to say that our need for membership remains unfulfilled there. It is, however, a space from which the experience of inherited culture, as that which guarantees social and moral identity, has all but vanished. People 'belong' to chat rooms and contribute to message boards. They join 'web communities' in which members share information concerning common interests. Still, there is nothing resembling a 'common culture' rooted in a shared past, one that serves as the foundation for a collective future.

Conventionally, it was through culture that communities expressed and celebrated their identity. At its most basic level, this manifested in established dress codes, etiquette and manners. By dressing in a certain way, and by expressing oneself in accordance with the generally accepted norms of behaviour, a person was not signalling an individual preference. If anything, he was identifying himself as someone bound to a particular people and cultural context. A person's style, in other words, was an expression of his attachment to place, a symbol of his solidarity with those who shared his values. However, the fact that formal dress codes and manners have collapsed suggests a loss of shared values. Portrayed as a victory for self-expression, it is, in reality, symbolic of self-loss and alienation from kith and kin. It amounts to a rejection of one's inherited identity and a refusal to be constrained by cultural norms. It signifies that we have nothing in common except our differences and that the 'I' has opted for exile over integration.

More broadly, it was through culture that a community attached itself to a particular place. Through careful planning and building, the landscape was designed in the image of its inhabitants, its architecture and monuments reflecting the community's spiritual aspirations and moral identity. No longer was this a purely 'natural' space; it was one which reflected a society's values and ideals. It expressed a right of ownership and a determination to prevail. It was, however, through art and music that settlement and communal values were celebrated and reinforced. Through poetry, painting, literature and song, people were united morally and emotionally. Art served to memorialise the origins of the community, to provide continuity and permanence in the midst of change and decay. That is why it was performed, celebrated and enjoyed publicly. People gathered to listen and recite in a way which reminded them that they belonged together and that their destinies were intertwined. In doing so, they drew from a repertoire of songs, poems and plays through which their sense of identity was endorsed.

The same cannot be said for those existing in Cyberia, where cultural experience is, once again, characterised by detachment and isolation. No longer is culture a celebration of common values, but something primarily enjoyed alone. People do not gather to rehearse and affirm the community's cultural identity; instead, music, literature and film are downloaded onto a machine and savoured in solitary confinement. We plug in so as to opt out. What once served to unite is now that which separates the individual from his society. If culture is disappearing from our world, if it no longer shapes and moulds the self, it is because it has been privatised. The advent of the iPod has resulted in the decline of a shared cultural life, the consequence of which is nothing less than social fragmentation. It also means that people no longer feel connected to the public space.

As we shall see later in this book, the purpose of art is not to unsettle. Nor should it celebrate alienation or displacement, for it is through art that we sensually and spiritually connect with our world. By capturing our longings and ideals in stone, on canvas or in song, it provides a sense of truth, reality and permanence. Hence, it is not surprising that when we are in exile from home – when we are physically, emotionally and spiritually disengaged – art and culture should reflect this. If, as Roger Scruton maintains, we have rejected beauty, it is because we have lost our deep sense of attachment and deserted the world. The result is that art now dwells on the ugly, on death and decay. It seeks to dramatise our estrangement from the world rather than celebrate our settlement. This explains why few can now identify with the sculptural monstrosities which currently dominate the skylines of most capital cities. This is art for the homeless, culture for the dispossessed.

A natural consequence of disconnecting from creation is separation from the Creator. As I point out in Chapter 9, the word 'religion' derives from the Latin *religare*, meaning to bind or to connect. As such, religion connects us to that which is greater than the individual self. In the first place, it binds us to our Gods and origins. It binds us to what Burke called 'the great primeval contract of eternal society',[9] to those who are living, dead and yet to come. Moreover, religion connects us to each other as fellow congregants and, in the case of Catholics, fellow communicants. In so doing, it supplies a form of membership in which all stages of life are consecrated and celebrated by the entire community. Through religion, we are bound by a common destiny forged from a common past.

The church, synagogue or mosque serves as a spiritual home, one which unites believers to the eternal. By serving as that 'point of intersection of the timeless with time', they also enable us to make a home for the Divine here on earth. Through the Church, God makes His presence felt among the community. He becomes, as in the Catholic Eucharist, the 'real presence', thus making it possible to directly commune with our sacred source. And, in becoming one with Him, we become one with all creation.

In the 'virtual kingdom' of Cyberia, we are never really present to others or ourselves. It could be argued that religion aims at virtual reality, that despite the centrality of the 'real presence', it is, in essence, concerned with the immaterial. At one level, it is certainly undeniable that religion is rooted in the immaterial and that it seeks to bind people spiritually. Unlike Cyberia, however, where people are not bound to anything but a machine, religion forms the basis of a real and concrete community. To belong to a community of believers is to be both physically and spiritually rooted to the real: real people, real places and real things. Through worship, congregants unite in a place where they believe the Creator has made His home. In partaking of Him, they become one body in faith.

Cyberia connects its 'users' through a World Wide Web, and yet no one is at home. Like the believer who worships at the tabernacle, that small portal through which worshippers make contact with their Creator, the Cyberian gazes silently into yet another small portal. What distinguishes the Cyberian from the believer is, however, that in seeking to unite with his sacred source, the religious adherent also seeks to unite with fellow believers and, indeed, with all others. The time he spends at the tabernacle, or before the shrine, serves to bind him more closely to his actual community. Communion, in other words, begets community.

Not so for the Cyberian. In a world where the tablet has replaced the tabernacle, there is nowhere for the Creator to take up residence. The 'real presence' becomes a perpetual absence, an open void from which all life has withdrawn. If religious worship sustains and strengthens belonging and community, the virtual kingdom destroys it. The sacred remains 'wholly Other'. This is reflected in abandoned churches and diminishing congregations across the Christian world. It is reflected in our refusal to sacrifice for absent generations by sustaining the legacy of the dead so that it will one day become a gift to their descendants. Nevertheless, in detaching from our sacred origins, we have not ceased to worship. What we worship now is, however, something which serves only to tear us apart.

These are the many themes which will preoccupy me throughout the remainder of this book. It could be said that my argument reflects a wistful longing for an old way of life whose time has come and gone. It could also be said that, notwithstanding all the obvious problems it presents, the age of Cyberia is a victory for liberty and happiness. Not only does it offer liberation from outdated custom and tradition, but it also affords a life of convenience, comfort and ease. No longer bound by place, time, God or nature, we have finally been released from the bondage of which Rousseau spoke when he declared: 'Man was born free, and is everywhere in chains.'

My response is simply to repeat what I have argued here and the truth of which I hope to prove in the remaining chapters: human beings cannot experience true freedom or lasting contentment by disconnecting from the world of which they are an integral part. They cannot live in a state of permanent exile and isolation, for to deny the real in favour of the virtual leads only to enslavement, alienation and addiction. That is why reconnecting with the real is the only way to be at peace with oneself, with others and the world. Either that or we are destined to remain forever homesick.

Notes

1　After writing this book, I discovered that a fellow philosopher, Hubert Dreyfus, had used the same concept in his book *On the Internet* (London: Routledge, 2001). Dreyfus has also written a groundbreaking critique of artificial reason in *What Computers Still Can't Do* (Cambridge: The MIT Press, 1992). As I develop it in this context, however, Cyberia is not exclusively a term referring to internet alienation, but also to that isolation and estrangement which liberalism and postmodernism, in all their manifestations, promote. My view is that we are not perpetually condemned to Cyberia but that there are many concrete ways to become reattached to reality. As such, the primary purpose of this work is not to emphasise our enslavement but to prove that there are always pathways home. Consequently, it is a work not of despair but of hope.

2　See Scruton, 'Hiding Behind the Screen' in *The New Atlantis: A Journal of Technology and Society*, Summer 2010. The New Atlantis is Published by The Center for the Study of Technology and Society and the Ethics and Public Policy Center, Washington DC.

3   The expression belongs to John Stuart Mill. See Chapter III,
    'Of Individuality, As One of the Elements of Well-Being', *Of Liberty*
    collected in Mill, *Utilitarianism* (Fontana Press, 1962), p. 185.

4   Aristotle, *Nicomachean Ethics*, trans. J. A. K. Thompson (London:
    Penguin Books, 1976), p. 271.

5   Søren Kierkegaard, *Two Ages: The Age of Revolution and the Present
    Age: A Literary Review*, trans. Howard V. Hong and Edna H. Hong
    (Princeton: Princeton University Press, 1978), pp. 92–3.

6   Kierkegaard, *Two Ages*, p. 104.

7   Kierkegaard, *Two Ages*, p. 74.

8   Michel Foucault, *The Order of Things* (London: Routledge, 1970), p. 387.

9   Edmund Burke, *Reflections on the Revolution in France* (New Haven:
    Yale University Press, 2003), p. 82.

2

Playing with our toys

The cry of a newborn is the howl of homesickness. Having been evicted from the womb, the infant is plunged into a strange world where he no longer feels at home. His screams are the sound of separation-anxiety, a primal expression of displacement and detachment. The world he confronts is alien and strange, a place with which he cannot identify. It is true that he belongs to a family and a nation. He has a name which attaches him to a particular history. The child is, however, totally impervious to all of this. Even when being slowly wrapped in the 'chains of custom', he is without any sense of self. Although conscious and having definite needs, he is neither *self*-conscious nor *self*-reflective. He cannot stand back from his immediate condition in order to reflect on his predicament. Being unable to conceptualise the world, it stands before him as something 'wholly other', forbidding and threatening. He is estranged, disconnected and displaced.

Moreover, the child is completely *dependent*. Contrary to the claims of Rousseau and his intellectual descendants, we are not born free. The nearest we get to the so-called 'state of nature', a state uncontaminated by society and culture, is when we first emerge from the womb. In that moment, we are, however, never more reliant on others to fulfil our needs. Basic instincts, such as hunger and comfort, must be satisfied by parents or carers. The child is enslaved to impulse, and his cries are a verbalisation of that enslavement. In reality, we are born in chains which can only be broken through education and integration into social, cultural, political and religious life. The institutions condemned by Rousseau are, in other words, the very basis of genuine liberty.

This process of emancipation begins as the child slowly starts to make his home in the world. At a certain point, he seeks to leave his mother's arms so as to engage with the immediate environment. If this signals the dawn of personality, it is because the child is striving to impose his will on something alien and strange. He is endeavouring to reconcile with something he previously feared. In so doing, he grasps the object, plays or toys with it. If our first real point of contact with the material world is through play, it is because play forms the basis of our early identity. In playing with a thing, the child surmounts the division between himself and object. It enables him to render familiar what was once threatening. By squeezing, banging and sucking on the object, he attempts to leave his mark on the world, to bend it to his will. At this primitive stage of development, the child is not *intentionally* confronting the world in an effort to understand it. He belongs to a sphere where everything is unfamiliar, and it is by playing with material things that he begins the long process of self-discovery. In the language of Chapter 1, it is through play that an infant first connects with, or attaches to, a world which will ultimately become his home.

If there is a sense in which we are born free, it is only in so far as newborn children have no understanding of limits or boundaries. Unless checked, they will toy with anything and everything. This attempt to literally 'ingest' the world is less a display of freedom than of primal anarchy. It is the lawless liberty of the megalomaniac who seeks to consume all before him. If, however, we do not condemn children as we would a megalomaniac, it is because we do not recognise their destruction as wanton anarchy. Rather, we interpret the headless flower, the smashed glass or the mucky handprints as signs of the very first stages of rational development. They are the birth pangs of personality, the natural consequence of a person *coming to grips* with their surroundings. In time, limits and boundaries will be established by the individual's parents. That, however, will not be a denial of freedom but a bridling of unbounded instinct without which genuine liberty would be impossible.

To play with the world is to make it your own. In childhood, we seek to take the strangeness out of things by possessing them. That is, our aim in playing with something is to dominate or make it 'mine'. It is to possess or own it, and it is through owning a thing that we make it our *property*. Consider a child playing with some wooden bricks. By placing one brick on another, he forms a structure such as a little house or a tower. Through play, he has thus begun to build, and in building he not only engages with raw materials but also shapes them in his own image. In so doing, he begins to identify those things as *his*. The fact that he does not actually own them is immaterial. What is important is that, through play, the child begins to leave his mark or spread his *personality* across the world.

There is, however, a big difference between play and *use*. To use a thing implies an understanding of what it is *for*. It presupposes that the user comprehends the *meaning* latent in the object. No longer is it perceived as having an independent identity over and above the use to which it is put by the user. Now, the identity of the object is determined by its role and function in a specific context. If infants have no sense of a thing's meaning, it is because they are not yet *language-users*. In philosophical jargon, we might say that their relationship to the world is not yet mediated through signs. Lacking knowledge of an object's definition, and thus its proper function, they tend to use it incorrectly. At this stage, therefore, there is still a significant gulf between children and their environment. Despite attempting to engage with the world through play, they are incapable of *recognising* themselves in it. Only when a child has learnt to speak, can he begin to correctly identify objects and to see how they ought to be used. At that point, the gulf between child and world is bridged. In answering to his needs, the world begins to seem less alien, different and strange. What was once a mere object is now something whose name and function is clearly understood. It has become something through which his self-identity is confirmed.

Take, for example, the case of kitchen cutlery. If we keep knives, forks and other utensils beyond the reach of young children, it is because they do not as yet understand their proper use. Like everything else, they are perceived as play items, things to be eaten, thrown or bent out of shape. In teaching children how to use such implements, we are not merely instructing them how to use basic tools. We are shaping them as *persons*, equipping them with vital knowledge that will, in turn, enable them to fit in to the world to which they belong. The correct use of a knife and fork permits the child to feel at home, to be accepted and affirmed as a member of his community. That is why the teaching of manners or etiquette is neither arbitrary nor optional. At its most basic level, etiquette is that by way of which a child learns to surmount estrangement. In learning how to use things in accordance with commonly accepted norms – that is, in learning how to dress, speak and act appropriately – children slowly acquire a sense of their true place in the world. They do so because they are affirmed as rational beings whose use of things is not merely functional but imbued with value. Indeed, if manners and etiquette serve as the basis for all subsequent education, it is because they provide children not only with a sense of a thing's practical meaning, but also of its *worth*. As such, they learn that we use objects as we do for a reason, one that is embodied in the very essence of the thing.

Table manners provide a good case in point. In preparing a table for a meal, we do so according to long-established patterns. First, we dress or decorate the table with linen cloths. We then arrange the cutlery at each place setting, ensuring each implement is appropriately positioned. Finally, we light a candle as a symbol of unity and belonging. To suggest that this is an arbitrary ritual, something which could easily be dispensed with, is to ignore the fact that each item on the table is there for a good *reason*. Each item is placed where it is, and performs the function it does, because it has been formed over time in response to our practical, aesthetic and moral requirements. We might say that each item embodies the personality (Hegel calls it *Geist* or spirit) of absent generations. By this I mean that each item is the product of a long history in which eating habits were refined, and tools carefully crafted, to satisfy those demands. Moreover, the customary conventions surrounding human consumption are not empty rituals but carefully construed practices modified and enhanced over time. This, again, was for good reason: in the first place, ceremony distinguishes human from animal consumption and, secondly, it enables us to regulate and coordinate our communal eating habits. If, therefore, table manners are essential, it is because they embody knowledge necessary for domestic and social harmony.

Consider, however, the consequences of not teaching children the virtue of table manners. In depriving them of such essential knowledge, parents delay their social, moral and personal maturity. They remain in a state of dependence, being, as they are, incapable of eating *independently*. They are, moreover, deprived of the social nourishment of sharing a meal, in as much as they fail to understand the norms which make that experience both possible and enjoyable. Consequently, they cannot identify themselves as full members of the community whose eating habits are regulated by those mores. If social and personal identity is forged through the correct application of such norms and values, it is because they serve as the very basis of membership. It is through them that a person is accepted and recognised as someone that belongs here as *one of us*. Etiquette implies a willingness to sacrifice or constrain individual impulse in order to accommodate the needs of others. It suggests a readiness to fit in so that others do not feel put out. Without it, we can never feel at home.

We are, however, living at a time when etiquette, manners and commonly accepted values are rapidly disappearing. In many cases, the TV dinner has replaced the traditional family dinner, thereby undermining the social aspect of eating and voiding it of its ceremonial content. As I suggested in Chapter 1, the advent of fast food has rendered eating a solitary exercise, a mere means to an end. Food is stuffed in rather than savoured, gobbled on the hoof rather than enjoyed with others at the table. The result is that people have become disconnected from that knowledge which is necessary for social coordination. They have, thereby, opted for alienation, fragmentation and separation, above identity, unity and belonging.

It seems to me that this fact reflects deep and profound changes in the institution of the family and in that of education. If Hegel defines marriage as a 'substantial tie', it is because both parties surrender their individuality to form a union consecrated by a solemn vow. It is, therefore, not simply a 'contractual relation' but one devoted to the reproduction and long-term maintenance of society. The family is, in other words, an institution dedicated not only to the propagation and security of children, but also to their formative cultural, moral and spiritual development. Recalling what I said in relation to etiquette and manners, it is through the family that a child's personality is formed; its function is not solely to nourish and safeguard the child's body but to provide the context in which that child comes to recognise itself as part of a greater whole.

Thus, children arrive in this world as strangers. To them, everything is alien, other and different. They are completely dependent beings, enslaved to impulse and instinct. Their initial efforts to struggle or play with the world result neither in knowledge nor in understanding but in a partial familiarity with objects whose true meaning remains concealed. Through the family, however, children acquire a sense of liberty and autonomy. In teaching them how to use things, how to speak and behave, parents enable their offspring to identify themselves as independent selves. They begin to perceive the world, not as something indifferent and unknown but as something useful and valuable. In disciplining their instincts and appetites, parents begin the process of *socialising* children, of making them feel at home with others. Real freedom is discovered, in sum, when children learn that they belong to a social sphere governed by commonly accepted values, one in which our own needs must be weighed against those of our neighbours. Only through moral discipline, in other words, can children escape the bondage of their natural condition.

All of this explains why recent ideological efforts to undermine the family are both misguided and dangerous. To suggest, as did left-wing psychoanalyst R. D. Laing, that 'families, schools, churches are the slaughterhouses of our children, colleges and other places are the kitchens,'[1] is to declare against freedom in favour of anarchy. It is to deny the necessity of those institutions through which we are connected to the world, our fellow citizens and absent generations. It is to argue that a child's identity can somehow be formed and shaped in the absence of parents, teachers and those who sustain the spiritual vision of humankind. In saying this, Laing was merely adding to the chorus of those who believe that the family is not a natural institution but an arbitrary construct in the service of power or oppression.

The best response to that is simply to highlight the social and behavioural problems which exist when children are failed by so-called 'dysfunctional' families and substandard systems of education. Those children do not experience a life free from, what Kenneth Minogue aptly described as, the 'worm of domination'.[2] If anything, they remain in a condition of alienation, estranged from themselves and society. Ironically, their predicament is often that of perpetual dependence: dependence on a State and a system against which they are constantly at war. Without any sense of membership, except with those whose identity is rooted in separation from the social order, they cannot be at one with others or at home in the world. This takes the form of opposition to, and resentment towards, everything that society considers legitimate and sacred. For how can you value or cherish something when you cannot recognise or identify it as yours? You cannot, which is why the principal purpose of the family is neither to dominate nor to suppress the child's freedom. Rather, it is to teach the individual how to overcome opposition and alienation by identifying himself as *one of us*. If that means the establishment of boundaries, it is because without them we cannot live freely and in peace.

Through moral discipline, the family emancipates children from *childishness*. In so doing, it enables them to engage with the world, not as an object of play or a thing to be consumed but as something worthy of love and respect. Note, however, that in attaching children to the social order, the family is simultaneously *preparing them to leave home*. The ethical education which children receive within the home is not an end in itself but one through which children discover that they are *persons* with rights and responsibilities. They are neither the 'property' of their parents nor the sum total of their natural instincts. Potentially, they are *self-conscious citizens* of an objective moral and social sphere. Family membership is, thus, a necessary but ultimately insufficient phase in self-development.

The primary purpose of parenting is to provide safety, security and love. Nevertheless, as children mature, that purpose becomes one of weaning them off their dependency on parents. It becomes one of teaching them how to adapt to the world so that it becomes less hostile. To 'bring up' a child means to instil those principles which will permit him to negotiate his way around the social sphere with ease. Children have a natural sense of this, expressed in their frustration with the world's refusal to bend to their will and in their impetuous desire to grow up. When, for example, children roar in response to an object which they cannot work, it is because they suddenly realise that they are still reliant on their elders. They scream because their quest for independence has been temporarily thwarted. If all children naturally aspire to surmount dependency, it is because they desire to leave behind their childhood and become full members of the adult world. They aspire to be recognised as independent agents who have made their home in the world.

To state that children have no desire to remain children might seem like an obvious observation. However, the prevailing emphasis on so-called 'child-centred' education has profoundly transformed the family dynamic. Instead of idealising the adult world, as that towards which children should aspire, the trend is to view the world of the child as an end in itself. The tendency is to bend the world to the child's needs, rather than orient the child towards something higher and nobler. When I was growing up, society was *adult centred*. In everything, we were reminded that, as children, ours was but a transitional phase towards the true goal of human life. Elegance, etiquette and serious education were the norm for those of our parents' generation, and it was this that inspired us to leave behind our 'childish ways'. Implicit in this was a rejection of Rousseau's notorious belief that 'the first impulses of nature are always right' and that 'everything is good as it leaves the hands of the Author of things; everything degenerates in the hands of men'.[3]

If that were true, it must follow that the first impulses of children must always be correct, and the efforts of parents to educate their children according to the established norms of society must be deemed a degenerate process. Notwithstanding the fact that most parents recognise this as a complete fallacy, it is now standard to emphasise the immediate interests of the child at the expense of his long-term requirements. Living in a child-friendly world, children grow up repudiating the responsibilities of adulthood. For theirs is a domain of games, gadgets and fun, one in which the hard labour of coming to grips with reality is rejected in favour of endless leisure.

To put it in a nutshell, what was once considered a primitive way of engaging with the world has become a standard educational model. The 'play theory of education', as Hegel called it, assumes that what is 'childish is itself already something of inherent worth and presents it as such to the children'. If, for Hegel, it was nothing of the sort, it is because in the eyes of children, 'it lowers serious pursuits, and education itself, to a form of childishness for which the children themselves have scant respect'. Its advocates may champion the child-centred approach as a victory for children's rights and self-expression, but in reality they 'represent the child, in the immaturity in which he feels himself to be, as really mature and they struggle to make him satisfied with himself as he is'. In so doing, they shield him to those ideals which, by prompting him to aspire to something greater, serve to liberate him from the bondage of childhood. That is, 'they corrupt and distort his genuine and proper need for something better, and create in him a blind indifference to the substantial ties of the intellectual world, a contempt of his elders because they have thus posed before him, a child, in a contemptible and childish fashion, and finally a vanity and conceit which feeds on the notion of its own superiority'.[4]

Self-knowledge may begin with play, but it does not end there. The family and school provide the context in which children overcome the homesickness of infancy by relating to the world, and each other, in a more engaged and rational manner. In doing so, the world becomes less an object of play and more a sphere of meaning. It is not that children cease to play but simply that they have transcended that stage in which it is their primary means of interaction and engagement. To prioritise play over work is nothing less than to sustain children in their infancy. It is to maintain their separateness from the social and political order which is their true home.

This suggests that the principal aim of education, whether at home or at school, is not to encourage children to be 'different' or 'alternative'. Naturally, all children have different aptitudes and talents, which are cultivated and perfected by parents and teachers. They are, however, refined according to commonly accepted rules which govern the practices in question. There are, in other words, standards of excellence in every sphere, in relation to which we assess the performance of children. Whether it is sports, academics or cultural pursuits, they are judged in line with objectively recognised criteria. Obviously, those who excel stand out but not in a way that separates them from the rest of the community. If they are considered different, it is only because they have excelled in a competitive situation and are, thus, publicly recognised as the best.

Cultivating difference for its own sake is not, however, the same as achieving excellence or distinction in a particular field. If anything, it is a way of separating the child from his community and peers. It involves forging an identity in defiance of conventional norms and disengaging from the world so as to pursue individual or arbitrary freedom. To 'opt out' in this way is, once again, to live a life of opposition and indifference to others. It is a condition of perpetual homelessness, one assumed by those who shun belonging in favour of isolation. This explains why, as conventionally construed, the aim of education is to shape the individual in light of the community's objective beliefs and practices. Its role is not to promote endless play and self-experimentation, which leads only to nonconformity and social alienation. It is, rather, to provide a context in which the child can, through sound learning, acquire a concrete sense of self-certainty and understanding.

In 'dumbing down' education, however, children remain immersed in immediacy. Through the introduction of child-friendly curricula, in which education is adapted to their current interests, children are not only severed from their past but fail to comprehend the world as an object of meaning. A knowledge-based curriculum comprises traditional subjects such as mathematics, classical languages, literature and history. In learning such subjects, children assimilate the truths distilled in tradition. As such, they learn how to differentiate subjective inclination from objective truth. By engaging with the wisdom of absent generations, the individual begins to understand *why* we do things as we do. With the dawn of reason, he sees meaning where once he saw only use. Through dialectical interaction with the past, he is united with his forebears and with their conscious attempts to make sense of their world. Uninformed opinion gives way to knowledge as the student begins to interiorise the 'best that has been said and thought'. In becoming acquainted with exemplary texts from the past, the student comes to fully comprehend and identify with the moral purposes of his predecessors. In so doing, he becomes a fully informed citizen who can intelligently interact with others and negotiate his way around the social world.

A child-friendly curriculum, on the other hand, is one that emphasises creativity or play at the expense of conformity. By 'conformity', I do not mean blind or unthinking devotion to a principle or cause. I mean, rather, an acceptance of beliefs and practices on the basis that they are rooted in reason and whose efficacy is established by long experience. The innovator, in other words, is not someone who abandons the wisdom of the past. He works in the light of what T. S. Eliot called the 'existing monuments', altering them only 'ever so slightly'. That, however, is not the object of a curriculum which aims to downgrade classical subjects in favour of fashionable alternatives or which seeks to discard time-honoured pedagogical devices, such as rote learning, in favour of child-centred techniques such as 'creative learning'. The effect of dumbing down classical subjects is not an education which will better equip students to flourish in the modern world but one which diminishes their sense of social, historical and moral responsibility. Creative learning which is not founded on 'existing monuments' risks alienating students from their past and thus from themselves. For example, it is now possible for Irish Second-Level students to leave school without having taken a single history class. This means they will graduate without knowing who they are or whence they came. Without the guiding light of historical knowledge, they will feel disengaged and detached from the political process. They will never truly belong.

A curriculum should unite and bind, and it should do so through knowledge. However, we no longer live in an age of knowledge but in a so-called 'information age'. The principal objective of the information age is not to enable the child to critically engage with or interpret his world. It is not to make him self-aware but to equip him with the requisite technical skills. In a world where people predominantly communicate through systems and screens, such skills are indispensable *but only at a certain level.* What they can never supply is the practical wisdom – Aristotle called it *phronesis* – which human beings need to flourish in a world of competing interests. That type of knowledge requires an education in virtue or the cultivation of one's capacity to respond appropriately to complex situations as they arise in the course of everyday life.

If the children of Cyberia are lacking in such knowledge, it is because those subjects which encourage self-reflection, and are replete with practical wisdom (history, philosophy, theology, classical civilisation and literature), are considered irrelevant or biased in favour of the 'established order'. This is reflected in the prevailing tendency to 'deconstruct' educational curricula so that canonical authors, poets and major historical events are either excised entirely or relegated to optional status. This refusal to distinguish between canonical and lesser authors means that students are incapable of discerning between, for example, Dickens and a contemporary novelist such as Dan Brown. The practical wisdom acquired in studying authors like Dickens is the reason for their greatness and their canonical status. This means that opting for Dickens over Brown is not simply a matter of subjective or individual taste. There are objective criteria which provide a solid basis for selecting Dickens or Shakespeare over some of their successors. These include the fact that those who study them are much more likely to come away enlightened as to the general requirements of virtue in their practical affairs. They are much more likely to know how to react and respond to unforeseen events which could otherwise crush them and those entrusted to their care.

What we know as 'information' cannot convey that type of knowledge. Acquiring information requires no critical reflection, self-awareness or interpretative capacity. In many ways, the information age is a natural corollary of the play theory of education. Its purpose is, as it were, to keep the person at play rather than answer to his 'genuine and proper need for something better'.[5] It is an age from which intellectual distinctions and hierarchies have all but disappeared. Hence, when a person searches in cyberspace for the answer to something, they are rarely led to the original source but drift from one subjective interpretation to the next. It is a world in which, as Nietzsche put it, there are no truths, only interpretations, one in which we are 'tossed to and fro and carried about by every wind of doctrine'.[6]

The result, as Benedict XVI so clearly identified, is that 'we are moving towards a dictatorship of relativism which does not recognise anything as for certain, and which has as its highest goal one's ego and one's own desires'.[7] The fact that we traditionally characterised children in such terms, as those who recognise nothing as certain and whose highest goal is their own ego and desire, suggests that childishness is now commonly accepted as our natural condition. It suggests that we regard leisure and play as the acme of human life. In so doing, we may believe we have become masters and possessors of nature, when in reality we have simply become enslaved to our toys.

Notes

1   R. D. Laing, *Politics of the Family* (Toronto: CBC, 1969), p. 35.

2   Kenneth Minogue, *Alien Powers: The Pure Theory of Ideology* (London: Weidenfeld & Nicolson, 1985), p. 226.

3   See Rousseau, *Emile* (New York: E. P. Dutton, 1968).

4   G. W. F. Hegel, *Philosophy of Right*, trans. T. M. Knox (London: Oxford University Press, 1967), p. 118.

5   G. W. F. Hegel, *Philosophy of Right*, p. 118.

6   St Paul, Epistle to the Ephesians 4:14.

7   Benedict XVI, Homily delivered on the eve of his election as Pope, 18 April 2005. See http://www.vatican.va/gpII/documents/homily-pro-eligendo-pontifice_20050418_en.html.

3

Dealing with the dead

If, as Benedict XVI contends, we are being swept along by every wind of teaching, if 'we are building a dictatorship of relativism that does not recognise anything as definitive, and whose ultimate goal consists solely of one's ego and desires',[1] it is because we are now witnessing *the triumph of liberalism*. In all its various forms, contemporary liberalism is a philosophy of homelessness and detachment. It repudiates tradition, custom and community, in favour of individual liberty unhindered by conventional constraints. It rejects local and national sovereignty while prioritising universalism, internationalism and globalisation. Having given up on God and Truth, it believes, following Protagoras, that 'man is the measure of all things', and that, as Nietzsche proclaimed, 'there are no truths, only interpretations'. Traditional morality, as that which provides objective criteria to distinguish between right and wrong or good and evil, is abandoned for an ethics of equality and social justice divorced from any theory of reality or human nature.

What is more, only those social and political arrangements which have been chosen or consented to by the individual are deemed legitimate. Prepolitical loyalties – to family, culture and religion – are routinely condemned as 'inauthentic', in as much as they encumber the individual with 'prejudices' not of his own choosing. Hence, as suggested in the previous chapter, family and religious obligations are generally abandoned by the liberal on the basis that they are inherited rather than rationally chosen.

In short, liberalism is a philosophy of rejection, repudiation and resistance to the established or traditional order. In refusing to be guided by what John Ruskin termed the 'lamp of memory', by a past from which they seek to twist free, liberals emphasise progress at the expense of permanence. For them, the future is that towards which we must constantly move, and we must do so through endless 'experiments in living', experiments in which we seek to remake society in our own image. For the liberal, this means that the true purpose of politics is not piecemeal reform but social revolution. Typically, that takes the form of ideologically vaccinating society against time-honoured beliefs and practices, beliefs to which the majority of citizens, in their hearts, still subscribe. Once again, the liberal justification for this is that those institutions which sustain timeless values – such as churches, privately funded schools, clubs and, indeed, the family itself – are enemies of equality. They are governed, in other words, by a hierarchical order with exclusive privileges. For example, the Catholic Church teaches that only men can be ordained priests because no women were present when Christ instituted the priesthood at the Last Supper. That is offensive to most liberals because, in their eyes, it contravenes equality. It neither matters that there is solid theological justification for a male priesthood nor that this teaching has existed for over two millennia. What counts for the liberal is that the Church, by violating egalitarian principles, has taken a stand against progress and must, therefore, be driven to the margins of public and political life.

In such a culture of rejection, one in which accepted authority gives way to unbridled experimentation, the individual is central. So, too, is the maintenance of his or her rights. Having condemned inherited obligations as mere 'prejudice' and with no established values to uphold, the individual inevitably sees his or her own ego and desires as the ultimate goal. That is why the rootless existence of Cyberia is a perfect domain for the liberal consciousness, one in which all concrete constraints on the individual have been swept away. In such a world, the only obligations are to oneself, to the fulfilment of one's own needs, appetites and impulses. It is a world in which possession is not determined by place, for it is an empty space, a no-place without limits. There are, however, consequences for abiding in a world without order, obedience and obligation, consequences described by Hegel in his enduring parable of master and slave.[2]

This parable, which Karl Marx used as the basis of his economic theory, is a prophetic account of liberal life in Cyberia. Let me provide a potted version of what I consider to be Hegel's greatest insight and one which shall serve as the basis of my subsequent argument. A master subjugates a slave, using him to satisfy his every whim. As the master luxuriates in comfort, the slave perpetually toils in the home and garden and on the land. What the master desires, the slave immediately supplies. Ostensibly, the master is lord of all he surveys, including the slave. He lives a life of ease, luxury and liberty, never having to work for the abundance he craves. Conversely, instant gratification is denied to the slave. He must diligently labour for everything he obtains, including whatever small degree of liberty he is afforded by the lord. To the outside observer, the slave's life is one of unremitting servitude in a world he cannot call his own. Owning nothing, he appears like an alien in a strange land, a person without home, freedom or value.

Appearances can, however, be deceptive. Without having to work or struggle for his possessions, the master derives no real satisfaction from them. The excitement of the 'instant hit', of the quick satisfaction of desire, soon subsides as the master lapses into a state of boredom and lassitude. He is, moreover, a stranger to himself and his surrounds. It is true that he owns his house and land, but having never practically engaged with, or worked on any of these things, he cannot recognise himself in them. He is an alienated observer of all he owns, someone who wants for nothing, but who, despite that, cannot find any lasting self-satisfaction. He is, furthermore, bound by the slave, in as much as the master is dependent on his servant for everything. The master is, in sum, enslaved to his slave.

While the slave cannot exercise his freedom, being as he is a 'possession' of the lord, he is, in many ways, more fulfilled than his master. Unlike the lord, the slave must actively engage with the world. In so doing, he achieves self-recognition through his work. In preparing the food, maintaining the house and tending the land, the slave shapes and moulds those things in his own self-image. They bear his stamp and reflect elements of his consciousness. If the lord accepts praise for his magnificent house and gardens, he cannot rightfully take pride in them. That is because they are devoid of *his* personality or consciousness. There is, as it were, nothing of the lord's self reflected in the things he owns. The slave, on the other hand, *can* feel a sense of pride because he recognises himself in and through his work. Despite having no claim to the land upon which he toils, he is fully at home in it. He has spread himself across its contours, thereby acquiring a concrete and lasting identity. This is the priceless self-knowledge for which the master longs, but which only the slave enjoys. As the master's relationship with the world is fully mediated through the slave, and because the slave has developed a sense of self denied to the lord, the so-called slave is, in reality, master of his master.

If this is a perfect parable for the contemporary age, it is because it underscores the illusion of individual self-mastery. The master believes he is fully self-sufficient, independent and free, when, in actuality, he is completely dependent on others to sustain him in his mastery. Consider once again the internet and how those netizens of Cyberia believe their virtual existence is one of pure liberty. Sitting alone before a screen, the Cyberian has unlimited access to everything and everyone. He can connect with the entire world, unhindered as he is by concrete constraints. Like the master, he can satisfy any desire at the push of a button. New identities can be forged and new communities joined without the need for lasting membership or long-term commitment. Indeed, the very notion of commitment is one that never features in Cyberia, for the individual self is sovereign. That is, the individual can pursue what he desires without having to make any personal sacrifices. If there is a morality here, it is certainly not a conventional 'we' morality, one which recognises that the needs of others must be balanced against our own. It is a space governed solely by a 'me' morality, one that exalts the ego and its desires above everything else.

Like the master in Hegel's parable, the Cyberian is a narcissist. Both appear to be stuck in what French psychoanalyst Jacques Lacan termed the 'mirror phase' of existence. According to Lacan, when young children observe themselves in a mirror, they over-identify with the image in an effort to compensate for their lack of bodily coordination and cohesion. The image becomes the basis of ego formation and self-consciousness. However, it is also the beginning of a narcissistic preoccupation with oneself, an over-identification with the image which can only be broken by engaging with others in the real world. The master desires recognition and so surrounds himself with objects that serve as multiple mirrors which reflect an image of self-sufficiency. Such objects affirm the lord in his sovereignty, thus convincing him that he can exist isolated and alone. The problem is that there is nothing behind the image – nothing real or tangible. The master's identity is purely spectral, whereas the slave, having died to the ego in order to engage with the world, acquires a genuine sense of self. The slave's identity is endorsed by the surrounding world that he has shaped. It has been actualised or concretised in the objects he maintains. It is true that the slave also sees himself *mirrored* in the world, but this is a reflection formed from the 'labour of death', the hard work of dying to the ego so as to earn the recognition of others.

Both the master and the Cyberian believe they can short-circuit desire. They believe that instant gratification and unlimited consumption are sufficient for the purpose of self-satisfaction. In staring at the screen, the individual sees only his own reflection. This is not what Hegel called 'identity amid difference', or identity that emerges through the mutual recognition between individual subjects. It is, to repeat, a narcissistic attempt to bypass others and the world in order to obtain recognition on the cheap. This can be clearly observed in the case of pornography, the purpose of which is to engage with others without actually engaging or to simulate sexual relations so as to avoid the effort of genuinely relating. In contrast to real flesh-and-blood people, whose consent for sexual relations must be earned, those on the screen can be used without having to acquire their consent. In this prison-house of mirrors, the aim is solely to satisfy the ego, something that virtual bodies can fulfil instantly and on demand. Once again, however, there is an illusion of mastery at work. The Cyberian who depends on pornography never achieves the lasting fulfilment that human sexual desire promises. To use Hegel's language, he never succeeds in attracting the desire of another, for the sole purpose of pornography is individual self-satisfaction. Consequently, he requires evermore 'hits' or quick fixes to satisfy the longing for real and lasting fulfilment, for the self-certainty that only true commitment can guarantee. Inevitably, this leads to dependency and addiction on the virtual substitute, a fact that proves his mastery is a sham and that he is, in reality, enslaved.

In all its forms, addiction alters reality, rendering it somewhat virtual. Those addicted to technology are enslaved to a virtual world divorced from reality. Likewise, the drug user and alcoholic seek to block out or numb themselves to actuality. The truth is, however, that you cannot bypass the real world entirely. There will inevitably come a time when the addict must face his addiction, a time when the 'user' comes crashing out of his virtual state and back into a world of real people who must then pick up the pieces. This is the moment when the illusion of self-mastery crumbles, when the individual suddenly realises that he is totally enslaved to that which he believed was the source of his security. The temptation inherent in all forms of liberalism – culminating in our postmodern culture of signs, screens, images and mirrors – is to assume that individual 'experiments in living' have no consequences for others or for society as a whole. So long as a person does no *harm* to others, what he does in his own space is his own business. If that is a dubious assumption, it is because, notwithstanding all attempts to repudiate somewhere for 'nowhere', individuals do not operate in a vacuum. They must live among others, and what they do will naturally affect or, in cases of addiction and licence, harm those people. The pervasive presence of pornography, and society's addiction to it, has, for example, led to a situation where the innocence of children can no longer be guaranteed. This seemingly private and harmless pursuit threatens, in other words, to undermine the very basis of sexual integrity and the life of virtue upon which society depends.

As applied to our own time, the truth of Hegel's extraordinary parable is this: However much people think they can detach from others and the world, however free, autonomous and self-reliant they believe they have become, the fact remains that we are mutually dependent beings. The master's liberty is an illusion because he is enslaved to the slave. His boredom and lassitude are symptoms of his failure to find genuine recognition, to establish an identity that is something more than an empty reflection. Like all those who seek to bypass the true demands of desire, he endeavours to dominate and control. In so doing, however, he only becomes more dependent on and subservient to the very thing that, in actuality, controls him. By contrast, the slave does not seek quick-fix recognition or affirmation. He understands that self-identity requires effort, the effort of engaging with others and the world until such time as you are affirmed by both. The effort of winning another's love, for example, demands dying to oneself so as to reach out to that person until such time as he or she reciprocates. Unlike pornography, which circumvents the process of attracting another's desire, genuine human relations are predicated on mutual affirmation, something which cannot be forced or obtained on demand.

If our world is one of alienation and estrangement, it is because it is addicted to instant gratification. What the ego desires it must have, *and have now*. Fast food, fast access and fast cars – all suggest a culture hooked on speed. To put it in a nutshell, we are all masters now. Hegel's great insight was that only through *delayed gratification* can human beings find lasting fulfilment. There are, in other words, no short cuts when it comes to making a home or a family or cooking a meal, which is why the home, the family and slow food have all been rejected by the liberal world. Neither is selfhood something which can be selected on a screen. Understanding who you are, and where you belong, requires a long detour through the residue of history and culture. That is to say, we all begin from where we are, but it is only by dying to the immediacy of infancy, so as to work on or grapple with what seems alien and strange, that you acquire an enduring sense of self.

This is best explained through the example of reading. A person sees a new book and desires to read it. In sitting down to do so, that individual dies to himself so as to become one with another, in this case the author. He engages with the material, analyses and learns from it. This is what Hegel means by the labour of death: the reader sacrifices his old self in order to enhance his knowledge and understanding by engaging with another's insights. In uniting his consciousness with that of the author, the reader enters an alien world. By the time he completes the book, however, the reader has absorbed its contents, thereby making familiar what was once strange. As in the example of the slave, the identity of the reader is established through concrete engagement with another, until such time as that other becomes part of oneself. 'Oneself as another' is how French philosopher Paul Ricoeur once described it, by which he meant that identity is not something readymade or chosen but an ongoing dialectical process which lasts a lifetime and in which others, both living and dead, feature fundamentally.

This, of course, is the central tenet of all conservative thought, one which sits at the heart of Edmund Burke's *Reflections on the Revolution in France*. When Burke wrote that great book, the Jacobins were laying siege to the cultural, religious and political patrimony of France. They were doing so in the name of 'liberty, equality and fraternity', the guiding slogan of all subsequent liberalism. However, in disconnecting France from her past, the Jacobins favoured the living above the dead and the unborn. Their aim was to destroy those established institutions which conserved the social, spiritual and historical capital for what Burke called 'absent generations'. This meant actively forgetting that ours is 'not a partnership in things subservient to the gross animal existence of a temporary and perishable nature', but a partnership 'not only between those who are living, but between those who are living, those who are dead and those who are to be born'. Burke called this 'the great primeval contract of eternal society'.[3]

Burke's essential point was that what we have, and who we are, is not something that *we* (the present trustees of society) make or choose. Rather, it is a *gift* transmitted from the dead to be conserved in trust for future generations. The gifts of the dead are embodied in our customs, values, institutions and cultural monuments, all of which pre-exist the individual and through which his sense of self is nurtured and formed. It is through these monuments that the dead continue to dwell among the living, thus ensuring intergenerational continuity. Deconstruct those monuments, however, and you sever the unborn from their 'canonised forefathers' and the world they created. You silence the voice of the dead, silence their wisdom as it is transmitted through the ages.

Conserving 'ancestral voices' is, therefore, a 'work of mourning' or what we might call a *labour of memory*. In recognising that we are the people we are only because others sacrificed on our behalf, conservatives faithful to Burke endeavour to temper their own desires for the sake of their descendants. This means safeguarding the cultural, moral and political ecology from plunder or decay. It means sustaining the gifts of the dead for the benefit of the living and of those yet to come. This, in turn, means acknowledging that we are products of the past (*oneself as another*), individuals whose identity is not of our own making but forged from the sacrifices of others. Repudiating the past, therefore, is nothing less than a repudiation of oneself.

At its best, conservatism is a philosophy of affirmation and preservation. Unlike those movements which revel in rejection, conservatism that is true to itself should refuse to disdain those things which have been handed down by our forebears. Rather, it should positively affirm them, recognising that in their absence we would be destined to a life without sense, identity or meaning. In dealing with the dead, however, there can be no immediate gratification or quick fix. The labour of memory demands constant vigilance, a willingness to die to one's own ego and its desires so as to dialectically unite with those in whose eternal shadow we stand. It suggests dying to one's own reflection, in the mirror or the screen, in order to see oneself as another and to affirm the other in oneself.

Cyberia is a domain of spectres and ghosts, a space in which communication is completely depersonalised. It is an immaterial world in which we exist without a trace. The real world beyond the screen is also somewhat spectral. In everything, there are multiple marks and traces of those who, like the slave, worked on those things to make them what they are. The world contains the consciousness, what Hegel again called the 'spirit' (*Geist*), of those who went before. Everything, in other words, has a history which is manifest in and through the object. If we can tell stories about our homes, belongings and artefacts, it is because they contain the spirit (*Geist*) of previous generations. They contain traces of the dead which animate them for the living. The dead, as it were, live on through their work and possessions.

A principal objective of the communist system, as indeed that of the Jacobins, was to exorcise the ghosts of the dead from the land of the living. It did so by attempting to scrape from the surface of the world all trace of the old order. Art, architecture and religious iconography were all drained of their character, smashed by the sickle until such time as the world could be redesigned in the image of the 'new socialist man'. The purpose of this vandalism was to disconnect the living from the dead, to empty the world of its spiritual (*Geist*) significance. In that way, or so the communists believed, the people would embrace the future instead of perpetually looking to the past as a guide to the present. Rather than genuflect before 'canonised forefathers', they would now become subservient to the State and its hollow promises of socialist utopia. By severing people from their heritage, they sought to deplete the storehouse of memory until such time as it no longer existed. At its most diabolical, this took the form of Pol Pot's 'year 0', in which the Cambodian dictator sought to erase all vestiges of human history.

As subsequent events proved, however, the spirit of the past is impossible to completely vanquish. No matter how hard the advocates of progress endeavour to silence the dead, we remain haunted by their ancestral voices. We can, of course, pretend that the dead do not dwell among us. Like the master, we can become convinced that we are what we make of ourselves, that we are fully self-sufficient. That, however, leads only to alienation and a false sense of identity. By contrast, when conservatives look at the world, they see an omnipresence of ghosts. For them, all objects bear witness to their creators. Even the so-called 'natural world' is imbued with consciousness, with the signs, traces and marks of those who planned, settled and worked on the surrounding environment. Understanding the world, and thus oneself, requires learning from the dead, incorporating their consciousness into one's own. As suggested in the previous chapter, the family and education provide children with their first glimpse of ghosts, their first encounter with a world shaped by absent generations and the debt they are owed. Hence, to undermine the family and traditional education is, once again, to detach from the dead.

That is why, in his denunciation of liberalism, Burke argued that a 'spirit of innovation is generally the result of a selfish temper and confined views'. Whether in politics, religion, culture or education, innovation for its own sake, or without reference to the past, serves only to wrench society from its moorings and to remake it on a whim. It is to assume that nothing can be learnt from the past that we, ourselves, do not already know. Just as the master is impervious to his dependency on the slave, so also the liberal is equally blind to the reality that he is a product of those he now endeavours to erase from memory. However, as Burke points out, 'people will not look forward to posterity, who never look backward to their ancestors'.[4] In ceasing to identify existing things as a bequest from the dead, one to be cherished and maintained for absent others, we come to see them as *ours* alone. It is then that we are tempted to do with them as we please, forgetting that they have been handed down in trust for future generations. It is then that we are tempted to see only our own reflection in the surrounding world, the spirit of our forebears having been eclipsed by the ego and its immediate desires. This is obvious in the case of the natural environment, which has been recklessly plundered without regard for those who seek to inherit the earth. But it is also evident in the manner in which we have either refused, or indeed failed, to maintain the social, spiritual and moral ecology of the species. Had absent generations been kept in view, we would have been far less likely to squander that precious heritage simply to satisfy the 'selfish temper' of its existing stewards.

None of this means that conservation is immune to innovation or that the spirit of the past cannot be adapted to the requirements of the present. In fact, innovation is necessary to tradition if we are to avoid, what T. S. Eliot calls, a 'blind and timid adherence'[5] to the past. What it does suggest, however, is that innovation must be tempered by 'the idea of inheritance [which] furnishes a sure principle of conservation, and a sure principle of transmission, without at all excluding a principle of improvement'.[6] To view the world under the aspect of inheritance means recognising that what we have is not ours by right but something handed down in sacrifice and love for safekeeping. It means caring for the gifts of ghosts, the legacy of those whose spirit lives on in and through creation and culture. It means treasuring that legacy simply because it does not belong to us but to our children. That is why conserving institutions, maintaining the civic, social and political structures which have been left to us, is not an option but an obligation. It is our way of acknowledging and honouring past sacrifices, those which were made on our behalf and which we, in turn, must continue making for those yet to come.

Hegel's entire philosophy is predicated on the insight that we can never surmount alienation, or find our way back home, unless we undertake the labour of memory. He called this process 'recollection', which is, in essence, a form or *resurrection*. In dying to one's immediate self so as to learn from others (present and absent) and the world, one is, quite literally, taking into oneself what is other, alien, strange and different. All knowledge, practical and theoretical, involves dialectically uniting one's consciousness with that of another. As such, we give new life to concepts and ideas which, if they were not passed on, could potentially fade from memory. The process of learning is, thus, one of recollection and resurrection, of establishing an identity in and through the dead. In assimilating or recollecting the spiritual legacy of others, we *revive, resurrect* and thus *sustain* it. Consequently, as Burke explains, we mould together 'the great mysterious incorporation of the human race', one that 'moves on through the varied tenor of perpetual decay, fall, renovation, and progression'.[7]

Liberalism has been often criticised for promoting a 'culture of death'. I prefer to say that it fosters a *culture of amnesia* or one of denial, in as much as it actively strives to forget the dead by cutting its links to the past. By driving the deceased out of our mind, we are thereby relieved of having to answer their summons to sacrifice. We no longer have to undertake the hard work of mourning, memory or recollection. And when that happens, we can simply ignore 'the great primeval contract of eternal society' between the living, the dead and 'those who are to be born'. We need only answer to ourselves, for life begins and ends with *us*. But that, once again, is to live in a condition of self-deception. For, it is only by recognising the dead and by honouring their sacrifices that we can establish who we are and where we came from. It is only by acknowledging that just as the master is nothing without his slave, so we are nothing without those who laboured hard so that we might live in relative ease. It is only by giving new life to our ghosts, by following their direction and continuing their work, that we can find our way back home.

To conserve is to remember and cherish with 'the warmth of their combined and mutually reflected charities, our state, our hearths, our sepulchres, and our altars'.[8] It is to gaze upon the world as one fashioned by our forebears, one abundantly imbued with their spirit and wisdom. It is to recognise that the rootless, self-sustaining identity which liberalism advocates is an illusion predicated on a denial of dependence, dependence on those who nurtured and shaped us. It is to foster a culture of thanksgiving in which we offer grace for all things, knowing that they bear the trace of those who sacrificed on our behalf. However, it also involves the responsibility to ensure that we uphold and maintain existing monuments so that others may one day enjoy their benefits.

When looked at in this way, we see that the core message of genuine conservatism is this: standing, as Eliot put it, at the intersection of 'the timeless and time', we, the living, serve to unite, in Burke's majestic words, the 'visible and invisible world'. That is why conservatism rejects rejection in favour of love: love of those absent others within oneself and of the world they bestowed to us: love of those others who depend on us for their survival and who, one day, will look upon us as *their* dead: love, in other words, of all those things which can never be made 'the object of choice', and which, when denied, lead not to 'progress' but to an 'antagonistic world of madness, discord, vice, confusion and unavailing sorrow'.[9]

Notes

1   See again http://www.vatican.va/gpII/documents/homily-pro-eligendo-pontifice_20050418_en.html.

2   See Hegel, *Phenomenology of Spirit*, trans. A. V. Miller (London: Oxford, 1977), pp. 111–19.

3   Burke, *Reflections*, p. 82.

4   Burke, *Reflections*, p. 29.

5 See T. S. Eliot, 'Tradition and the Individual Talent', in *The Sacred Wood: Essays on Poetry and Criticism* (New York: Alfred A. Knopf, 1921).

6 Burke, *Reflections*, p. 29.

7 Burke, *Reflections*, p. 29.

8 Burke, *Reflections*, p. 30.

9 Burke, *Reflections*, p. 83.

4

A work of love

Only human beings are capable of love. That is because, unlike other creatures, only we recall the past and anticipate the future. Stating it philosophically, only we can ask the question of being, of the purpose and meaning of life. That question is provoked by the knowledge that, one day, we shall die. Animals have no such conception and so they live in blissful ignorance of their ultimate fate. They neither mourn, in the human sense of perpetually grieving for a past which will never again become present. Nor do they have a sense of their own extinction, a sense that, at some point in the future, they will no longer exist. If life has urgency for us, it is because, as German philosopher Martin Heidegger put it, we are 'beings-toward-death'. Our lives are haunted by the prospect of loss. We know that life is limited and that nothing lasts eternally, that a place has already been reserved for us among the ranks of the dead. Therefore, we cling to what we have while we still have it. This awareness of death is what prompts us to love and cherish life, but it also helps us to identify with, and conserve the memory of, those who have gone before. Drive death out of mind, however, and the first casualty is love. It is then that life is deprived of its urgency. In living in and for the moment, we favour 'temporary little arrangements' over long-term commitments.

All love involves sacrifice. It involves tempering the ego and its desires for the love of another. That is why both Hegel and Kierkegaard considered marriage fundamental to the ethical or moral life.[1] In marriage, two people sacrifice their individuality in order to unite as one. They *vow* to remain united until separated by death. This vow is nothing less than a covenant with absent generations. It is a proclamation before the entire community that theirs will be a common future forged from a common past. It is a pledge to those long gone that their bequest will be sustained and transmitted to those yet to come. The vow of love is, in other words, a promise of sacrifice for the living, the dead and the unborn. This explains why, within the Christian context, marriage is considered a *sacrament* or an earthly channel of Christ's eternal grace. Marriage ensures the transmission, not only of the 'deposit' of faith but also of what is 'ours' thanks to the sacrifices of others. It unites the generations in seamless harmony, thus guaranteeing the conservation of values hard won but too easily lost. Defined thus, marriage is a 'work of love'.

People connect in Cyberia, but they almost never commit. As I remarked in the previous chapter, Cyberia is a loveless zone haunted by spectres and chimeras but devoid of the dead. It is a space where users look neither forward nor back because they are rooted solely in the instant. Hence, it is a world where the concept of sacrifice has no meaning or application. Even still, you do not have to log on to Cyberia to see what happens in the absence of sacrifice. In forgetting the dead, and in severing marriage from its sacramental context, contemporary liberal society has lost the impulse to sacrifice. Recalling Burke's warning that people 'will not look forward to posterity, who never look backward to their ancestors', we can say that it is because people no longer have any sense of their past that they fail to sacrifice for the future.

This is obvious in the prevailing obsession with perpetual youth. Instead of following the example of our ancestors, who perceived themselves as but a single phase in an intergenerational conversation, we seek to shut down that dialogue in order to cling steadfastly to what we possess. In resisting the idea of growing old, and in seeking to conceal any sign of age, we are, in effect, refusing absent generations a right to their patrimony. If loving involves sacrifice, and if sacrifice has been largely rejected by the present age, it is no surprise that committed love, and marriage as the institution which fosters and sustains it, has also been rejected.

Without love, however, nothing can be sustained. In its absence, as Burke rightly predicted, everything collapses into 'the dust and powder of individuality'. We act as though we were 'the entire masters' and thus 'commit waste' on our inheritance. In failing to honour and respect the institutions of our forefathers, in failing to conserve and transmit their gifts, we shall 'leave to those who come ... a ruin instead of a habitation'.[2] That is why, as I have been suggesting, *nothing motivates those of a conservative temperament more than love*: love of family, home, society and even the State. Consequently, their principal conviction is to conserve those institutions which cultivate the impulse to sacrifice and the motive to love. Their primary purpose is to care for the legacy of the dead so that it may survive beyond the present generation.

If, therefore, 'family values' are of considerable concern to conservatives, it is not because they wish to impose on society the outdated norms of a bygone age. Rather, as I remarked in Chapter 2, it is because without marriage and the family, the wisdom of the past (moral, religious, political) cannot be handed down. To repeat: implicit in the vow of marriage is a promise to the dead that they shall not be forgotten. As such, it is through the ordinary routines of domestic life, routines ordered by sacrifice and love, that children first become aware that they dwell among their departed.

The family home is a place, not only where children learn how to survive in the world but one in which their memory and identity are first formed. It is there that they begin to identify with their forebears, and they do so through stories and narratives told by their parents. Out of love for their children, parents invoke the dead, cite their example and explain why it is necessary to emulate it. Thus begins the long labour of memory and mourning, without which self-knowledge would be impossible. If conservatism is a work of love, it is because it is predicated on a promise never to forget. Unlike the culture of amnesia, which revels in repudiation and rejection, conservation sustains and cherishes the memory of inherited things. Consequently, in bringing up their offspring with a sense of who they are and whence they came, parents simultaneously nurture the motive to sacrifice. In teaching children *respect*, they rescue them from the mirror stage of existence and the narcissism of youth. In effect, they impart the *virtue of reverence*: reverence for the dead, the living and those who will come in their wake.

That is why bringing children up is not just a matter of caring for their body. It is much more a matter of caring for their soul. By this I mean that children have more than physical needs: they also have a moral sense which, if not properly nurtured, will result in their being what we aptly call 'spoilt'. To spoil children is to indulge their every whim to the point where they seek to satisfy only their own desires and impulses. It is to encourage selfishness at the expense of self-restraint or indulgence at the expense of sacrifice. The upshot is that a spoilt child will look no further than the present and will spare no thought for anyone but himself.

The antidote to such egotism is respect, reverence and responsibility. To respect and revere something is to see in it much more than one's own reflection, something more than a means of satisfying one's own immediate desires. It is to perceive it as possessing a life of its own and a summons to sacrifice. When, for example, I show respect for another's property, it is because I see something of that person in it. Likewise, in revering an ancient artefact, I consider it animated by the presence (what I earlier referred to as 'spirit') of our ancestors. It is this which serves to curtail consumption and egotistical desire, for it is considerably more difficult to consume something when it contains traces of life.

If the social order is under strain, it is primarily because the world is now widely perceived through a purely functional lens. It is not to be revered and respected but is there solely for *our* pleasure, purpose and use. Respect and reverence have become prime victims of the culture of amnesia, a culture in which children are impervious to the presence of their canonised forefathers. The result is a decline in social accountability and good manners and a general disengagement from anything which comes between the self and its own reflection. It is a culture of egoism in which we, the living, are indeed considered the 'entire masters', and in which our social, moral and spiritual ecology is now a ruin rather than a habitation. It is, moreover, a culture of rights practically devoid of all responsibility, in the sense that we no longer *respond* to those who laboured and sacrificed on our behalf.[3] We can no longer hear their call through a cacophony of ceaseless noise.

Writing in *The Human Condition*, Hannah Arendt noted: 'what love is in its own, narrowly circumscribed sphere, respect is in the larger domain of human affairs'.[4] As defined, respect is a way of cherishing and affirming others and the world. It is, as Hegel says, 'a sensing of something living', something with which I am invited to identify. Hence, when an object appears lifeless and derelict, it serves to alienate people. That is simply because we are tempted to disrespect those things with which we cannot identify. However, in sensing that something is living, that it still bears 'the stamp of our forefathers',[5] we are more likely to honour and respect it. We are more likely to care for and thus to 'domesticate' it. If respect goes hand in glove with responsibility, it is because both are ways of *responding* to the world, not as something to be used for our immediate gratification but as something worthy of conservation and love. Implicit in respecting something is an acknowledgement of our debt to those whose spirit it embodies and a promise that we shall strive to preserve it for the benefit of our progeny.

It may be too much to say that the widespread loss of respect is due, in large part, to the concomitant decline in the sacramental idea of marriage. The fact remains, however, that in the absence of an institution which links the living to the dead and the unborn by way of a solemn vow, it is inevitable that people will begin to see only themselves mirrored in their surrounds. It is inevitable that respect and the virtue of reverence, without which there can be no work of love, will cease to characterise the moral life of society. Without an institution dedicated to the conservation and transmission of memory, in other words, it is unavoidable that our dealings with each other and our world will be transformed beyond recognition. For when we cease to mourn, we simultaneously cease to love, sacrifice and respond to the requirements of others. As with the master in Hegel's parable, we become dedicated solely to the self, vanquishing all opposition in the process.

In such a society, people cease to look back simply because they do not know how. This means that, in as much as they are divided from the dead, they cease to mourn. As both Freud and Ricoeur suggest, 'mourning is a reconciliation' with objects of love. Hence, if love and sacrifice are to function as guiding principles, as that which restrains the ego and its desires, there must be a solemn 'duty to remember'. This means the work of mourning is not something we do only when those whom we love perish. As 'heirs of the past', it is something we must first learn to undertake as children. For, it is through mourning that we are reconciled with our heritage, reconciled with that through which we discover a lasting sense of identity. There is, as Ricoeur says, 'a kind of erosion which strives to bring everything to ruins, to ashes'.[6] That kind of erosion can take the form of wanton cultural vandalism, such as that inflicted on France by the Jacobins, or it can simply happen because we refuse to remember.

To plug in to Cyberia is to disconnect from the dead. Still, the culture of amnesia is not confined to cyberspace. Consider, for example, the architecture of the postmodern city, where monstrous glass towers each vie for the supremacy of the sky and where flickering billboards dominate the streetscape. In such a city, there are few traces of the dead. It is a city of mirrors in which we, the living, see only reflections of ourselves. By reconfiguring the city so that it retains no element of tradition, the dead are evicted from their home among us. They are driven out of sight and thus out of mind. This is a city built solely for present purposes, for the needs of a generation that never sleeps, never reflects, never mourns. As described by Jacques Derrida, whose influence on the world of architecture has not been inconsiderable, 'this architecture called deconstructive … begins precisely by putting into question everything to which architecture has been subjugated, namely the values of habitation, utility, technical ends, religious investments, sacralisation, all of those values which are not in themselves architectural'.[7]

This, however, is to deny the essential motivation for all building. To borrow Heidegger's terminology, we build in order to establish a permanent dwelling here on earth.[8] In so doing, we pour ourselves into the world, so that it begins to reflect our deepest hopes and longings. The purpose of architecture is not, therefore, to alienate us from the world but to enable us to *root* ourselves in it. It is to build a home which will last and which will, contra-Derrida, embody the values of habitation, technical ends and religious investments. The principal purpose, in so doing, is to enshrine and transmit to future generations the ideals and values of their predecessors. As Roger Scruton explains in respect of sacred architecture:

> The stone of the temple is the earthly translation of God's eternity, which is in turn the symbol of the community's will to live. The temple, like the liturgy contained in it, is 'forever'. The community is not of the living only, but contains the dead and the unborn. And the dead are protected by the temple, which immortalises them in stone.[9]

If postmodern architecture unsettles and disrupts, it is because it repudiates the very idea of home, belonging, settlement and memory. It is a space from which the spirit of the past has been entirely exorcised. By erasing from our common dwelling all memorials to the dead, it prioritises rupture over continuity. However, following John Ruskin, we can say that while we might be able to exist in the absence of traditional or classical architecture, 'we cannot remember without her'. This is why, he continues, 'it is in becoming memorial or monumental that a true perfection is attained by civil and domestic buildings'. As I will discuss in Chapter 8, civic buildings ought to embody, and thus reflect, the enduring values of a nation. They ought to bear witness to the origins of that nation, its struggle to prevail and its will to persist. Consequently, they ought to inspire the affection and admiration of all citizens. For these buildings enshrine our common identity, shared history and our collective sense of purpose. Think, for example, of Buckingham Palace or St Paul's Cathedral in London, both of which speak of a country's continuity despite historical change. They are monuments to unity amid difference, conveying as they do a sense of the timeless in the midst of time. If the English people cherish those buildings, it is because they remind them of their ancient settlement and thus the debt they owe to their dead.

Ruskin condemns as an 'evil sign' when people build their houses 'to last for one generation only'. He does so because, from his perspective, a house is nothing less than a temple, one in which 'it would make us holy to be permitted to live'. As distinct from those that rise on their ruins, a home that is built to last is one that speaks to us of sacrifice, honour and suffering. If we grieve at the prospect of such a home being 'swept away', of a time when no respect will be 'shown to it, no affection felt for it', and no good to be drawn from it by our children, it is because all that we have ever treasured will then be 'dragged down to the dust'. Domestic homes are, however, not meant to satisfy the 'little revolution' of one's own life, not meant for 'present delight, nor for present use alone'. They are not meant to alienate but to bind us to the past, to bind us to an inheritance ingrained in stone.

Hence, as Ruskin concludes, the greatest glory of a building is 'in its Age, and in that deep sense of voicefulness, of stern watching, of mysterious sympathy, nay, even of approval or condemnation, which we feel in walls that have long been washed by the passing waves of humanity'.[10]

Architecture that follows long-established patterns provides a domicile for the dead among their descendants. It is way of building which memorialises and preserves the spirit of absent generations. That is because it speaks of neither transience nor decay but of continuity and stability. Moreover, it represents a summons to sacrifice short-sighted aspirations for the community's long-term survival. To drain buildings of their 'values of habitation' or their 'religious investments' is not just a way of 'liberating' architecture from the crust of convention. More significantly, it severs their inhabitants from the true source of their identity. Once again, the primary purpose of building is to establish a home that will survive and which exemplifies the values of its past and present occupants. Our homes and buildings speak of who we are and what we cherish, which is why a home should always reflect its owner's values of habitation and religious investments. It should signify how they relate to the earth, their ancestors, neighbours and the wider community. If such homes give concrete witness to these things, postmodern structures are indicative of detachment, rootlessness and a refusal to commit to anything beyond the moment.

Homes link the generations, which is why Burke argued that 'the power of perpetuating our property in our families is one of the most valuable and interesting circumstances belonging to it, and that which tends the most to the perpetuation of society itself'.[11] The family home is both a repository of memory and a site of sacrifice. It is, as it were, a concretisation of the vow of love which binds us to the dead and the unborn. It is a symbol of lasting commitment and a declaration of our long-term settlement. In seeking to 'disfigure' architecture, postmodernism is making much more than an aesthetic statement.[12] In building with glass and wood rather than stone, and in rejecting customary patterns, postmodern architects insist they are pushing conventional boundaries in the name of what is 'different' and 'other'. Following Derrida, they perceive architecture as something which must always be open to the novel and unexpected. From their perspective, traditional architecture is merely a 'construction' that endeavours to house what is 'radically other', thus making it subservient to the same.

The fundamental message of postmodern architects is this: instead of trying to domesticate the dead, instead of trying to memorialise them in stone, we should simply surrender our ghosts. As such, the way we build should reflect loss rather than stability, absence rather than presence. It should extinguish the 'lamp of memory' in favour of 'the catastrophe of memory', or of that which cannot be truly mourned or recollected because 'there is nothing that remains of it'.[13] In denying that we can domesticate our ghosts, postmodern architecture seeks to redesign both the civic and living space in such a way that they are rendered porous, permeable and open to the future. We must live, not in the light of eternity, but in the silhouette of the unexpected, the strange and the monstrous, which Derrida describes as that which 'frightens precisely because no anticipation had prepared one to identify this figure'. If the future is 'necessarily monstrous', it is because it is that 'for which we are not prepared'.[14]

To plan a city or a house according to such logic is to disregard the established norms of settlement, belonging and the very idea of home itself. It is one thing to apply it to the relatively abstract sphere of academic discourse but quite another to impose it on the tangible human world. That is because, as Hegel understood, people cannot flourish when their lives are threatened by such uncertainty. Without experiencing acute alienation, as a result of which they become detached from the ties that bind, people cannot live with both eyes on a future that heralds the incoming of the unfamiliar and the monstrous. To do so is to build solely to shock, as indeed so many civic and cultural buildings now do. Expressing a rejection of the past in favour of what is to come, they stand as objects of alienation rather than of love. Whereas conventionally structured buildings sought to make people feel at home, their postmodern counterparts seek only to disturb, disorient and disenchant. Such is the nature of the monstrous.

Still, even Derrida believed that we must be prepared to 'accord hospitality to that which is absolutely foreign or strange … to try to domesticate it, that is, to make it part of the household'.[15] Humans are natural homebuilders. We desire a solid sense of identity which can only be realised by shaping the world in our own image. In so doing, we domesticate what is different, identify with it to the point where it becomes known and recognisable. Once again, this is what Hegel called 'identity amid difference' or a sense of identity which recognises that we are not self-sufficient but mutually reliant beings. Hence, just as there is an illusion of mastery, it is equally illusory to believe that we can live without a home or without being able to render familiar what appears, initially at least, as strange, alien, other or different. It is an illusion to think that we could happily live in a society, or adapt to structures that aimed at 'the destruction of memory itself', that rejected monuments, memorials and holy abodes in favour of 'an absolutely radical forgetting'.[16]

As Derrida put it, 'love is narcissistic'. By this, he meant that without the ability to recognise something of the self in what is other, true love would be impossible. That explains why we love and thus conserve old buildings, family homes and heritage. Naturally, there is much in our political and social history, much in our own personal narratives, which will have been lost to memory. This, however, does not relieve us of the responsibility to remember what we can so that the dead might one day connect with the unborn. While this will involve incorporating, or housing, the dead among the living, this does not necessarily involve reducing them to the same. Only in those cases where the past is plundered in the interests of a political movement, such as fascism or extreme nationalism, will the memory of our dead be so reduced. In the normal course of human affairs, our desire to retain and conserve is, however, motivated by a deep longing to identify with people without whom we would not be. It is motivated by a desire to be reconciled with the objects of our love.

To live in constant anticipation of the future is to risk forgetting that the dead ever existed. In being forever open to the strange and unfamiliar, we risk remaining strangers to ourselves. Hence, it is simply mistaken to claim, as do many postmodernists, that the work of mourning is a form of 'repression'. If anything, it is the purest form of hospitality of which we humans are capable. As Kierkegaard writes, the 'work of love in recollecting one who is dead is a work of the most unselfish love'. That is because the dead cannot repay the love they are afforded. In offering them a habitation, in conserving their legacy, in worshipping at their shrines and preserving their monuments, we are not seeking to repress but to honour those who cannot reciprocate. Likewise, when we sacrifice for the unborn, we do so for those we most likely will never know and who can give nothing in return. To conserve is to offer the most generous hospitality to the other in myself. And if this counts as an 'eternal duty', it is because in recollecting the dead 'you will also have the best guidance for rightly understanding life'.[17]

It is, of course, easier to forget than to remember, in as much as forgetting involves neither work nor sacrifice. Simply by 'plugging in', it is possible to drown out the appeal of absent generations, possible to deny them hospitality. By remaking the world in its own image, the culture of amnesia has brought to fruition that 'kind of erosion which strives to bring everything to ruin, to ashes'. Ash, as Derrida writes, is something that 'testifies to the disappearance of memory', to the 'destruction of memory itself'.[18] It is a sign that something has been effaced, in the sense that it is no longer recognisable. When fire consumes a thing, that object loses its form and is considered alien and strange. Essentially, fire disfigures and destroys. In defacing the world, the vanguard of the culture of amnesia engages in a work, not of love, but of 'destruction'. This is a kind of cultural and spiritual holocaust in which the face of the world, a face painted by our predecessors, is set alight and disfigured. Forgetfulness is the furnace in which such a sacrifice takes place, a furnace in which our memories are reduced to ash.

Ash, however, is a trace that can lead *somewhere*. It testifies to the fact that something once stood where now there appear only ruins. It suggests that even though a place may seem to have been irredeemably destroyed, it is not without its living secrets. As I remarked in Chapter 3, however much we try to drive the dead out of our mind, they have deposited their traces everywhere, even if they have now been reduced to smouldering cinders. Thinkers such as Derrida believe that where there is ash, 'mourning is not even possible'. However, they also argue that this leads not to nihilism but to affirmation: an affirmation of that which resists memory or recollection. We should not, they claim, attempt to resurrect or domesticate our ghosts, but, as in the example of architecture discussed earlier, we should simply release them. To do so, however, is to risk forgetting that we have forgotten – that radical form of 'forgetting of which nothing remains'. It is to risk total detachment from the past and thus from ourselves. And if that is not a risk worth taking, it is because it is an indulgence the unborn simply cannot afford. By evicting our ghosts, we do nothing less than disinherit their descendants. The duty to recollect the dead is, therefore, 'an imperative directed towards the future'.

Even when confronted with ash, we must, as Ricoeur insists, fight against the 'erosion of traces'. Indeed, conservatism believes that 'all human activity is a kind of counter-trend which endeavours to see that growth prevails over destruction, and that traces and archives are kept alive'.[19] That is why it is a message of true love and affirmation, a paradigm of genuine hospitality and generosity. It affirms that the world was not made by us but by others who are thus worthy of our respect and reverence. Those 'others' are manifest in and through their work – in which their wisdom is enshrined – and also in the very fabric of the institutional life of society.

In sustaining those institutions, and in passing on that wisdom, conservatives serve the cause of growth over destruction. This, however, does not mean that conservatism resists change or merely conforms to the canons of the dead. It acknowledges that the past comes down to us as a collection of traces which we must interpret from our present perspective. Nevertheless, in contrast to their liberal and postmodern opponents, conservatives perceive in all traces of the past a 'real presence'. Whereas liberals affirm absence, loss, difference and otherness, conservatives consider it a duty to resist the 'catastrophe of memory' by affirming the presence of the dead in all they have left behind. Only in this way can we hope to avoid the alienation and estrangement which the postmodern world, typified by Cyberia, seems to value as the condition of true freedom.

In countering the culture of amnesia, conservatism seeks to reconnect to the past as something living, as something which calls out to us to be remembered, revived and renewed. After all, who has ever walked and laboured on this earth in the hope that one day they shall be forgotten? Who goes to the isolation of the grave hoping they shall not be recollected? Who, even in a culture dedicated to destruction, wants to disappear without a trace? Conservatism believes that not even the legionnaires of liberalism desire such a fate. This is why, as we shall see, its objective is to respond with love to 'the world which made us', to sacrifice for its survival even when it has been reduced to ash.

Notes

1 See Kierkegaard, *Either/Or Vol. II*, trans. Howard and Edna Hong (Princeton: Princeton University Press, 1990). For Hegel's philosophy of marriage, see *Philosophy of Right*, pp. 111–22.

2 Burke, *Reflections*, p. 81.

3 See Chapter 6.

4 Hannah Arendt, *The Human Condition* (Chicago: The University of Chicago Press, 1974), p. 243.

5 Burke, *Reflections*, p. 73.

6 Paul Ricoeur, 'Memory and Forgetting', in Richard Kearney and Mark Dooley (eds), *Questioning Ethics: Contemporary Debates in Philosophy* (London: Routledge, 1999), p. 10.

7 Jacques Derrida, *Points...*, trans. Peggy Kamuf and Others (Stanford: Stanford University Press, 1995), p. 214.

8 See Martin Heidegger, 'Building Dwelling Thinking', in Heidegger (ed.), *Poetry, Language, Thought*, trans. Albert Hofstadter (New York: Harper & Row, 1971), pp. 145–61.

9 Roger Scruton, *The Classical Vernacular: Architectural Principles in an Age of Nihilism* (Manchester: Carcanet, 1994), p. 108.

10 John Ruskin, *The Lamp of Memory* (London: Penguin, 2008), p. 14.

11 Burke, *Reflections*, p. 44.

12 As an example of how postmodernism seeks to disfigure architecture, and the religious consequences of doing so, see Mark C. Taylor, *Disfiguring: Art, Architecture, Religion* (Chicago: University of Chicago Press, 1992).

13 Derrida, *Points...*, p. 391.

14 Derrida, *Points...*, p. 387.

15 Derrida, *Points...*, p. 387.

16 Derrida, *Points...*, p. 209.

17 Kierkegaard, *Works of Love*, trans. Howard and Edna Hong (Princeton: Princeton University Press, 1995), p. 358.

18 Derrida, *Points...*, pp. 208–9.

19 Ricoeur, 'Memory and Forgetting', p. 10.

5

Fantasies of freedom

The aim of all philosophy is to put us in touch with truth and reality. Since Plato, its principal objective has been to shatter appearance or illusion in order to reach what philosophers sometimes call the 'really real'. In a famous parable, Plato describes a scene where people are imprisoned in a cave. Burning behind them is a fire which projects shadowy images onto a wall, which the prisoners mistake for reality. When one of their group escapes from his chains and ascends into the light of the sun, they realise theirs is a world of illusion and fantasy disconnected from truth. One purpose of this parable is to remind the philosopher of his proper calling, which is to labour in the service of truth. It is to draw us away from the shadows and into the light of reality, where we shall see ourselves as we truly are.

Escaping from the shadows means overcoming illusion, fantasy and the chimera of the cave. It means moving from the fake light of the fire into the warm glow of the sun. It demands that the prisoners cease conflating their own reflection with reality, looking instead to the one true and lasting light. Such is the process of self-understanding, a process which begins in darkness and ignorance but which ends in knowledge of what is real, true and enduring. Plato believed that truth could not be discovered in the material world, which he compared to a cave-like sphere of illusion. Rather, it is to be found in an extrasensory world of essences or what he described as 'forms'. Hence, in order to arrive at genuine knowledge of truth, we must nourish reason or the soul at the expense of the body. In contrast to the flesh, the soul is immortal and indissoluble, an epiphany of truth in an otherwise fading world.

When viewed from our perspective, there is much to reject in Plato's thought. Still, his belief that philosophy ought to lead us from appearance to reality is one that has animated the subject down the centuries. In whatever guise, the philosopher's function was to deliver people from ignorance and alienation to an understanding of what is genuinely true, good, just and beautiful. Today, however, we live in a world which shuns reality in favour of fantasy. In a radical inversion of Plato's parable, not only have we shifted our gaze from the sunlight, but we have also descended back into the cave firmly securing the entrance stone in the process. Cyberia is, of course, a land of multiple shadows, illusions and phantasms. As I have argued, it is a virtual space devoid of genuine communication, knowledge and grounding in truth. It is a world in which the individual ego feeds off multiple fantasies in order to sate its immediate desires. Nevertheless, in bypassing the requirements of reality, fantasy convinces those addicted to it that they are 'masters of everything'. This is because the phantasm on the screen, being totally compliant, poses no threat or resistance and makes no demands. To repeat what I said in an earlier chapter, the image can be turned on and off at will and is but a means to unlimited self-satisfaction. In such circumstances, it is inevitable that one should ask, 'What's the use of truth?'[1]

As if to provide philosophical justification for our retreat into the land of shadows, that question has become commonplace among the cave dwellers' postmodern heirs. In fact, it serves as the basis for that popular movement known as pragmatism, whose high priests include American thinkers William James, John Dewey and Richard Rorty. Rorty's basic contention was that there are no areas of culture which are more successful at getting in touch with reality or truth than any other. That is because all experience is 'linguistically mediated'. By this, he meant that we come to know ourselves and the world through language, and there is no way of setting language aside to discover the true nature of the world or the self. There is, in other words, no reality lurking behind appearances, no 'way things really are' apart from the way we humans describe them. Consequently, the descriptions of the world deployed by the priest are no more or less accurate than those used by the scientist. With no way to come between language and the world, no way to test how accurately various descriptions *correspond* to reality, we ought to 'replace the appearance-reality distinction by that between descriptions of the world and of ourselves which are less useful and those which are more useful'.[2] The obvious rejoinder is 'useful by what standard?' Rorty's reply was simple: 'useful to create a better future' for, as Dewey wrote, 'growth itself is the only moral end'.[3]

In the name of freedom, progress and growth, Rorty urged that we simply cease trying to access truth, reality and eternity. Invoking Shelley's idea that 'the poet's function is to glimpse the gigantic shadows that futurity casts upon the present', he writes that 'we should just forget about the relation between eternity and time', concentrating instead on that 'between the human present and the human future'. 'Utopian social hope' is what motivates the pragmatist, one which is 'obsessed by the possibility of the disclosure of new worlds'. Rorty's deep wish is 'for everything to be wonderfully, utterly changed', which is why he recommends that we 'take full advantage of people like Luther, Copernicus, Galileo, Darwin and Freud'. This is not because they have made a unique contribution to the cause of truth or because they have advanced our understanding of reality. For all the reasons stated above, their genius did not consist in getting behind language to see what the world is really like. Rather, with their novel and original descriptions, they gave us 'our chances to transform the candidates for truth and thereby make previous patterns of justification obsolete'.[4]

The implications of this are clear: if what we call 'truth' is merely a more useful description, one that serves *our* particular purposes, then there is nothing enduring in the human condition. There is nothing of lasting worth in the wisdom of the past, simply because it comprises a set of useful descriptions which, having served their purposes, can now be replaced by better descriptions. On this view, we cannot claim that any of the great philosophers brought us into direct contact with truth or reality. Rather, they were merely 'strong poets' who dreamed up new descriptions (Rorty also called them 'vocabularies') which enabled our forebears to solve some of *their* problems. None of them could be said to have discovered 'The One Right Description', in as much as there is no way of juxtaposing their particular description of reality against reality itself. Only if there were such a way could we say with certainty that the insights of the past were something more than, as Rorty described them, 'metaphoric redescriptions'. There is, however, no such way because words are not like mirrors which accurately represent reality but are more like tools which help us to cope with the surrounding world. When faced with new problems, it makes no sense to depend on old and useless tools. In such circumstances, we must invent new tools which will help us make progress.

To follow Rorty is to see contingency at the heart of every-thing. Selfhood, community and even language are all provisional and can be redescribed as the need arises. Whereas traditional philosophy considered *reason* as the faculty which could, by transcending appearances, reach reality, the pragmatists emphasise the role of *imagination*. However, as defined by Rorty, imagination is something 'shared by all of us relatively leisured language-users – all of us who have the equipment for fantasy'.[5] Accordingly, imagination is a faculty for dreaming up new vocabularies or descriptions which, while not putting us in touch with the truth of things, can lead to envisioning ourselves and the world anew.

As I see it, Rorty's project cannot survive his conflation of imagination with fantasy. For him, the strong poets were those whose private fantasies eventually 'caught on' and became accepted wisdom. At first, their novel descriptions were greeted with disdain, ridicule or even shock. Think, for example, of how Christ's Gospel of love was received by the Jewish authorities or how Galileo was treated by the Inquisition. According to Rorty, those and similar 'poets' did not discover something essential about the intrinsic nature of reality, truth or the universe. Rather, their strange-sounding fantasies ultimately became the dominant vocabularies of succeeding generations, but only because they happened to serve *their particular purposes*. They disclosed unforeseen worlds, thereby making everything new. From this perspective, all the so-called 'great poets' *were* indeed fantasists. For the essence of fantasy is that it detaches us from reality, thereby tempting us to believe there is nothing outside of ourselves to which we owe obedience. Pragmatism is, thus, a philosophy of detachment which denies the sun beyond the cave, asserting that the flickering, ephemeral shadows are all we have. As Rorty wrote in his last book before his death in 2007:

> To give up the idea that there is an intrinsic nature of reality to be discovered either by the priests, or the philosophers, or the scientists, is to disjoin the need for redemption from the search for universal agreement. It is to give up the search for an accurate account of human nature, and thus for a recipe for the Good Life for Man. Once these searches are given up, expanding the limits of the human imagination steps forward

to assume the role that obedience to the divine will played in a religious culture, and the role that discovery of what is really real played in a philosophical culture.[6]

Once again, this is to confuse fantasy with imagination. If fantasy disconnects us from reality, the imagination, as Roger Scruton remarks, is 'informed by a sense of reality'. That is to say, imaginative emotions 'arise out of, and are controlled by, an understanding of the world. And to exercise this understanding is to take an interest in truth.'[7] Of course, it may well be that this use of 'world' and 'truth' does not correspond to what Rorty has in mind when, for example, he declares 'there is no one way the world is' or that 'truth is not the goal of inquiry'. However, they *do* correspond to what we generally mean when we use those words. Scruton argues convincingly when he writes that the 'world for us is *our* world. It is identified within experience, by using methods intrinsic to human reason. Since these are the only methods we possess, it is futile to reject them. Besides, this rejection undermines the critical task, which is to define the areas in which the distinctions between appearance and reality, and objective and subjective, make sense.'[8] In other words, *our* use of 'truth', 'world' and 'reality' cannot be put in doubt without fundamentally undermining what it is to be human, what it means to feel at home in the human world. Hence, what Rorty defines as imaginative disclosures of new worlds is best described as *fantasies of freedom*.

This, of course, is not to suggest that imagination cannot disclose new possibilities or that it must remain resistant to the future. What it does imply is that it cannot become detached from actuality, or indeed the past, without collapsing into fantasy. If it is to supply something more than 'empty utopias', it cannot totally transcend the 'field of experience' or the realm of reality. When Rorty states that he longs 'for everything to be wonderfully, utterly changed', he is merely repeating the catch cry of a litany of liberals who, since the French Revolution, have sought to destroy the past in the flames of their hollow fantasies. If he believes that 'an ideal liberal society is one which has no purpose except freedom ... no purpose except to make life easier for poets and revolutionaries',[9] it is because, in thinking of the past as nothing more than a mere contingent product of 'idiosyncratic fantasies', Rorty succumbs to what Richard Kearney rightly labels 'a naive affirmation of progress'.[10]

Rorty was by no means a revolutionary, but he did have what I call a 'revolutionary temperament'. By this I mean that, like most liberals, he was not content with mere reform but sought effective emancipation from tradition. If such fantasies of a brave new world are naïve, it is because in 'banishing the past to the shades of oblivion',[11] they deprive us of the practical experience and knowledge we require to navigate our way into the future. To return to a point I have made repeatedly in these chapters, we belong to history and to a particular tradition before we can set about reforming, revising or rejecting it. We are moulded and shaped by a past we have not chosen and are, therefore, in debt to those whose bequest our heritage is. Hence, language speaks through us before we master it, which is to say that, even before birth, we have a name, a history and an identity.

We belong, that is, to an ongoing historical narrative, one to which we are reconciled by memory and recollection. To suggest that this is somehow a contingent construct which, in the name of an unknown future, can be redescribed beyond recognition, is not freedom but illusion. It is to deprive oneself of the very resources required to build a concrete future from the sediment of the past.

The conservative imagination does not work in the service of a nebulous future but begins from where we are. The world itself – reality – provides the content of its thought-experiments. As I have been saying, this world is comprised of fragments and traces which bear the imprint, or the consciousness, of our predecessors. The purpose of education is to overcome the distance between past and present, by rendering familiar what was once alien or strange. It is to make one's own that which initially appears foreign or unfamiliar. Whereas the liberal views the past as nothing but a dead letter, one to be discarded for a formless future, conservatives see it as offering our best chances for 'social hope'. By reconnecting with the world of our ancestors, we can apply, what Burke called, 'the latent wisdom' which prevails therein. In understanding why they did as they did, we can thus adapt their wisdom to our present and future purposes. We might say it is a process which requires going back to the future.

Imagination allows us to bridge the distance between past and present. In a literal sense, we cannot revive the dead. Through imagination, however, we can enter their world and make sense of their motives, actions and decisions. Such is the work of biography and history, a process which refigures the past so as to render it intelligible and plausible for those of us living in the present. The historical imagination does not fantasise about the past but builds a coherent and credible narrative around relevant texts and traces. Its task is to put shape and meaning on what ostensibly appears disjointed and discordant. In so doing, a world opens up before us, one that is rooted in the fragments of a past reality but which has been *reconfigured* through imagination. The fact that we must use imagination to fill in the gaps and holes of history is precisely why Derrida speaks of a 'catastrophe of memory' and the 'impossibility of mourning'. However, traces and texts are not mere shells without a living core. They contain within themselves the spirit (*Geist*) of their authors' intentions and are a perpetual invitation to recuperate what has grown silent only in form but never in content.

In a literary culture, such as ours has always been, the world of the past constantly informs that of the present. Through stories, songs and myths, the reader or listener temporarily suspends his or her place in the living present so as to follow the narrator elsewhere. The purpose of this is not to escape reality but to *transform* it. By imaginatively engaging with the 'world of the text', a new horizon of possibilities opens up before the reader. Through imagination, the wisdom latent in the work becomes a reality which can then be appropriated as a guide to life. That is why the traditional bedtime story for children is not just a luxury but a necessary component in their social and moral development. Through imaginative variation, they exist alongside characters that embody a whole range of virtues and vices, thereby learning how to distinguish between them. However, in a society dominated by the image, nothing is left to the imagination. It is a fantasy world of false idols, one which can convey nothing deeper than itself. The image on the billboard or the screen can be bought, possessed or consumed in an instant. Hence, it is a perfect icon for the culture of amnesia, a culture at war with objective reality and 'the long-term view of things'.

In seeing traces and texts as a permanent sign of human intentions, the conservative imagination rejects the common assumption that tradition is 'an inert transmission of a lifeless residue'.[12] If anything, it contains within itself the 'spirit' of the past, a spirit which continually speaks to those prepared to listen. Tradition offers to the present generation a repository of wisdom, one which can light the way to a future grounded in something more than idiosyncratic fantasies and intellectual pipedreams. If such dreams are dangerous, it is because they are the product either of what Burke called 'naked reason' or of visions so distinctly divorced from reality that they barely conceal their contempt for the lives of ordinary people. That said, the conservative imagination does not seek to remain perpetually rooted in the world opened up through engagement with the past. The purpose, to repeat, is to tap the resources of the past in order to make sense of the present and to build a common future. Paul Ricoeur states it well when he writes that to 'give people back a memory is also to give them back a future'.[13] It is to give them the ability to see in a shared past the capital from which they can forge a destiny rooted in something more solid than the specious ideals of the revolutionary or the postmodernist poet.

This means that while the conservative imagination is faithful to the past, ensuring that it is neither forgotten nor subject to ideological distortion, it is no less faithful to the future. However, this is not a shapeless future in which 'everything is wonderfully, utterly changed'. Rather, it is one founded on concrete realities which have stood the test of time. If they have survived this test, it is because those realities are not immune to modification, innovation or change. Change is not a word generally favoured by conservatives. They follow Michael Oakeshott in believing that 'change is a threat to identity, and every change is an emblem of extinction'. But they also know that changes 'have to be suffered, and a man of conservative temperament (i.e., one strongly disposed to preserve his identity) cannot be indifferent to them', the reason being that unless the wisdom of the past can be adapted to the needs of the present, it will simply degenerate and die. Unless it can respond to unforeseen problems, it will cease to serve as a reliable guide towards a stable future. Still, if change or innovation is not to swing free of the past, and thus become the motor of some dangerous delusion, it must respond to 'some specific defect, one designed to redress some specific disequilibrium'.[14] Recalling the insight of T. S. Eliot, '[f]or order to persist after the supervention of novelty, the *whole* existing order must be, if ever so slightly, altered'.[15]

In sum, the conservative imagination avoids dissolving into fantasy by working within the existing order and never losing sight of reality. As bequeathed by absent generations, the world is not something inert or lifeless. It is one shaped in response to specifically human needs, to their physical, cultural and spiritual requirements. It is a world of meaning which contains within itself 'the general bank and capital of nations and ages'. The purpose of interpreting or putting order on the past is not solely to see where we have come from but also to identify or unite with that past. The whole notion of self-identity is, thus, undermined when we go forward without first looking back. To possess a sense of the meaningfulness of the past is the primary precondition for an understanding of self which is more than a mere provisional or contingent construct. This, however, is not a 'closure to what is new' but a process which 'preserves the meaning that is behind us so that we can have meaning before us'.[16]

The new Jacobins are motivated by an idea of progress as radical rupture from the past and thus from the given reality of our lives. Where conservatives see the spirit and consciousness of absent others, radicals see only a barrier to untried and untested fantasies. In seeking to 'disrupt the familiarity of the features of his world', the liberal/postmodern revolutionary seeks to unmask the present so as to reveal the skeletal remains beneath. He strives, as Scruton puts it, to strip away the 'skin of significance' from the world, thereby exposing its desiccated entrails. As a so-called 'master of suspicion',[17] his aim is to deconstruct all those things which make us feel at home (history, custom, culture and religion), seeing them as nothing more than 'stuffed birds in a museum'. Of such people, Burke wrote, 'With them it is a sufficient motive to destroy an old scheme of things, because it is an old one. As to the new, they are in no sort of fear with regard to the duration of a building run up in haste; because duration is no object to those who think little or nothing has been done before their time, and who place all their hopes in discovery.'[18] Burke wrote that prophetic sentence in 1790. Two hundred years later, and 'the enlightened among us' continue, in their various ways, to tear old things down simply because they are old. But those things with which they are replaced, and which are invariably run up in haste, are welcomed only by those who, according to Oakeshott, 'esteem nothing, whose attachments are fleeting and who are strangers to love and affection'.[19]

The conservative imagination is characterised by love: love of all those things with which we are familiar and which give sense and meaning to our lives. It is not a 'mere idolising of what is past and gone' but a way of looking at the given reality which sees it as something precious because it contains the seeds of our future happiness. It is to see the 'subjectivity of the world' and to respond to it with affection, knowing that it contains all that is necessary to keep alight the flame of hope. Thinkers like Rorty long for 'a global, cosmopolitan, democratic, classless, casteless society', one whose inhabitants will have severed all attachments to heritage and home. However, that is to prefer the unknown to the familiar, the untried to the tried, mystery to fact, the possible to the actual, the unbounded to the limited, the distant to the near, the superabundant to the sufficient, the perfect to the convenient, utopian bliss to present laughter.[20]

If utopians prefer future bliss to present laughter, it is because they cannot rest content with reality. Those like Rousseau, Marx and Nietzsche sought comfort in fantasies not of this world. They looked instead to a nebulous nowhere, one in which humanity would finally be emancipated from what they considered as its chains. And when, as in the case of Jacobinism and Communism, they attempted to make that nowhere a somewhere, the result was neither bliss nor laughter but slaughter and mayhem. Conservatives do not seek after bliss, an emotion they consider best suited to other-worldly visionaries. In being attached to this world, and to all those things that make it lovable, they do however make time for laughter. This laughter is not merely an 'expression of amusement' but one of satisfaction at having found a place they can call home, and upon whose foundations rests the only future worth having.

Notes

1   See Richard Rorty and Pascal Engel, *What's the Use of Truth?* (New York: Columbia University Press, 2007).

2   Rorty, *Philosophy and Social Hope* (London: Penguin Books, 1999), p. 27.

3   John Dewey, *The Later Works 1925-1953*, vol. 12. (ed.), Jo Ann Boydston (Carbondale: Southern Illinois University Press, 1987), p. 181.

4   Rorty in Józef Niznik and John T. Sanders (eds), *Debating the State of Philosophy* (Westport: Praeger, 1996), p. 52.

5   Rorty, *Contingency, Irony, and Solidarity* (Cambridge: Cambridge University Press, 1989), p. 36.

6   Rorty, *Philosophy as Cultural Politics* (Cambridge: Cambridge University Press, 2007), p. 104.

7   Scruton, *Modern Culture* (London: Continuum, 2000), p. 59.

8   Scruton, *Philosophy: Principles and Problems*, p. 39.

9   Rorty, *Contingency, Irony, and Solidarity*, p. 60.

10   Richard Kearney, *Poetics of Modernity: Toward a Hermeneutic Imagination* (New Jersey: Humanities Press, 1995), p. 82.

11   Paul Ricoeur, *Time and Narrative, Volume 3* (Chicago: The University of Chicago Press, 1988), p. 215.

12   Paul Ricoeur, 'Life in Quest of Narrative', in David Wood (ed.), *On Paul Ricoeur: Narrative and Interpretation* (London: Routledge, 1991), p. 24.

13   Paul Ricoeur, 'The Creativity of Language', in Richard Kearney (ed.), *Dialogues with Contemporary Continental Thinkers* (Manchester: Manchester University Press, 1984), p. 28.

14   Michael Oakeshott, 'On Being Conservative', in Roger Scruton (ed.), *Conservative Texts* (London: Macmillan, 1991), p. 245.

15   Michael Oakeshott, 'On Being Conservative', in Roger Scruton (ed.), *Conservative Texts*, p. 87.

16   Ricoeur, 'The Creativity of Language', p. 22.

17   This phrase was first coined by Ricoeur.

18   Burke, *Reflections*, p. 75.

19   Oakeshott, *Conservative Texts*, p. 242.

20   Oakeshott, *Conservative Texts*, p. 243.

6

The law of the home

Liberals, Cyberians, utopians and postmodernists are all united by the fact that they long to sever their domestic ties. They reject the local in favour of the universal, the familiar in favour of anonymous global networks. They deny borders, boundaries and distinctions, for a worldwide egalitarian fraternity liberated from the 'oppression' of custom, convention and tradition. In so doing, they eschew the 'economy' – a word deriving from the Greek *oikos*, meaning household, and *nomos*, meaning law. For conservatives, the 'law of the home' is something sacred, something that ought to be sustained and cherished. For their opponents, it is but one more instance of power which must be resisted in the name of unbridled freedom. It does not matter that all those who profess disdain for this law have been shaped by it. Neither does it matter that they were born, not as liberal individuals or as global citizens but as people belonging to a particular place defined by local laws and customs. The crucial thing is that, in order for such freedom to flourish, those laws and customs must be subject to consistent and sweeping critique. Burke summed it up well when he said of those 'enlightened' liberals who would put old France to the flame: 'Their attachment to their country itself is only so far as it agrees with some of their fleeting projects; it begins and ends with that scheme of polity which falls in with their momentary opinion.'[1]

If conservatives seek to uphold the law of the home, it is because they consider it neither feasible nor desirable to transcend it. Hence they defend the local over the universal, the familiar over the anonymous. Their attachment to their country is founded on reverence and fidelity to that place which made them, and whose geography, law and culture constitute the fabric of their identity and the object of their true affection. Liberals and postmodernists sometimes respond to this by condemning conservatives as nationalistic, chauvinistic or xenophobic. The nation, they claim, is an 'artificial' entity that prioritises 'us' over 'them', the selfsame above the stranger. According to postmodern philosopher John D. Caputo, such 'nationalist identitarianism does everything it can to prevent the "other" from crossing over "our" borders, from taking "our" jobs, from enjoying "our" benefits and going to "our" schools, from disturbing "our" language, culture, religion, and public institutions. [It] could not be more inhospitable to the coming of the other.' In contrast, the postmodernist yearns for 'highly heterogeneous, porous, self-differentiating quasi-identities, unstable identities … that are not identical with themselves, that do not close over and form a seamless web of the selfsame.'[2]

When postmodernists, and indeed liberals, speak of the 'other', they generally mean non-Westerners. Accordingly, the nations of the West, those of Europe and the United States, are 'the almost perfect embodiment of "identity", of identitarianism, of self-affirming, self-protecting, homogenising identities that make every effort to exclude the different'.[3] The irony is, however, that the only countries which actively seek to suppress difference are those which constitute what postmodernists label 'the other'. The tyrannies and theocracies of the Middle East, for example, are the almost perfect embodiment of self-protecting identity. Strangers and outsiders must rigidly conform to local norms, while 'minorities' are almost completely suppressed. There is no room for protest or intellectual inquiry which strays beyond that which is sanctioned by the authorities. There is, in other words, no functioning civil society in which citizens can freely engage in artistic, cultural or intellectual pursuits without fear of punishment. If anything counts as an example of 'domination' or 'power', this is surely it. And yet, in the eyes of its liberal intellectuals, the West is something akin to a giant prison in which citizens are unwittingly enslaved to a system of surveillance and punishment. Again, following Rousseau, their contention is that although born free, we are everywhere in shackles.

French philosopher Michel Foucault wrote of the subtle ways in which we are 'disciplined' through our participation in institutional life. The family, Church and the political order are all instances of power which serve to limit the liberty of the individual, to 'govern' him as it were. In fact, from Foucault's perspective, this is a more insidious power structure than the naked power exercised by the tyrant. Whereas those opposing the tyrant can identify the source of their subjugation and resist it accordingly, the coercion exerted by institutions is almost undetectable. It masquerades as a 'civilising' force, one which people consider essential to freedom, success and happiness. As such, the 'modern State' is a 'new form of pastoral power' which, according to Foucault, is that form of power traditionally exerted by the Christian Church. As he wrote, pastoral power 'cannot be exercised without knowing the inside of people's minds, without exploring their souls, without making them reveal their innermost secrets. It implies a knowledge of the conscience and an ability to direct it.'[4]

All the institutions of the modern State, such as 'those of the family, medicine, psychiatry, education and employers', exercise 'pastoral functions' which serve to control and subtly coerce 'individuals'. Consequently, the objective should not simply be to 'liberate the individual from the State' but to resist the State and that 'type of individualisation which is linked to the State. We have to promote new forms of subjectivity through the refusal of this kind of individuality which has been imposed on us for several centuries.'[5] Put simply, what we define as 'individuality' is yet another manifestation of pastoral power and must, therefore, be equally resisted if genuine subjectivity is to be realised.

Foucault was a citizen of a State which provided him with unrestricted space and freedom to develop his critique of 'power relations'. His books, which sought to 'unmask' the sophisticated power structures at work in society, circulated freely and without official censorship or condemnation. He was never imprisoned for his views or forced to recant. Indeed, as an intellectual superstar, he taught widely in Europe and the United States, enjoying the abundant fruits of a system he equated to a police state. In many ways, his very existence undermined his basic thesis, for where else outside of the West would someone like Foucault have flourished? For example, those Middle Eastern intellectuals who take issue with their political order are routinely imprisoned, persecuted or worse. Only in a system which permits dissent, critique, eccentricity and difference could an intellectual write and speak as. Foucault did. His resistance was against a 'system' that permits and encourages resistance, one that allows contrarians of any persuasion to question the legitimacy of 'the system'.

What I am suggesting is that the Western political order is anything but the pure 'totalitarian unity' condemned by leftist intellectuals in the mode of Foucault. If anything, it is an order founded on consent and one which lets all flowers bloom. It is a self-revising entity which, when confronted by discrimination or bigotry, reforms its laws so as to prohibit prejudice against what is perceived as 'different' or 'other'. It makes room for deviance, defiance and dissent, for novelty, originality and innovation. It allows artists and intellectuals to challenge established conventions and boundaries, to push imagination and inquiry to their limits.

What is more, it seeks neither to silence nor to suppress those voices which speak from the margins of tradition. Counter-cultural philosophers, historians and artists are provided with a platform from which they can 'deconstruct' the canon, thus 'liberating' the work of those who seek to 'unsettle' and 'disturb'. Only in a system which recognises difference will difference thrive, which is why, contrary to what those like Foucault maintain, the West is porous, self-differentiating and hospitable. Only there are foreigners and strangers welcomed and permitted to live in accordance with their traditional norms and values. The proof of this is the fact that whereas few migrate from the West to settle elsewhere, vast numbers migrate from elsewhere to settle in the West. And they do so to enjoy the benefits of a system which, in contrast to their own, is both welcoming and affirming of their so-called 'otherness'.

There are, of course, many reasons why the nations of the West are open, hospitable and self-revising, but two in particular are worthy of mention: the Judeo-Christian inheritance and the ideals of nationhood. The Judeo-Christian character of Western countries takes the form of respect for secular law and the democratic institutions which sustain it but also of peace, forgiveness and justice. Christ's injunction to love the enemy, to forgive others their faults and to withhold nothing from 'the least of these my brothers', underpins modern democratic politics. Rather than serving as the origin of 'pastoral power', this 'law of love' has served to ensure a political order rooted in tolerance and charity. It is true, of course, that many atrocities were carried out in the name of Christianity and that much suffering was inflicted on the stranger and the slave beneath the banner of the Cross. However, it is equally true that in the absence of the Judeo-Christian tradition, the West would not have become, both within and beyond its frontiers, a champion of freedom in opposition to those who would deny it.

John Caputo says that we 'need to avoid both the overtly self-enclosing, isolationist, protectionist nationalisms and also the crypto-nationalism of thinking "we" are the exemplary case'.[6] But where in the West are such self-enclosing nationalisms? Nazi Germany and fascist Italy were, of course, perfect examples of this, but these were countries against which the rest of the civilised world took up arms. More recent examples beyond Europe were Saddam Hussein's Iraq and Bashar al-Assad's Syria. North Korea is another striking illustration. In contrast to such benighted places, the nation states of Europe and America are paradigmatic cases of what Derrida calls an 'open quasi-community', one whose identity 'begs to differ with itself'.[7] While there are political parties and groupings (such as Sinn Fein in Ireland) which espouse nationalist, communist or even revolutionary ideology – what Burke called 'armed doctrine' – the politics of Europe and America is not animated by self-enclosing or inhospitable nationalism. It is not a jingoistic politics, as Caputo says, that is 'built around a defence that a "we" throws up against the "other"'.[8] Rather, it is a 'we' that welcomes 'others', makes them feel at peace and allows them to seamlessly integrate as common citizens. Nowhere else on this planet are people so free to move with ease, so free to come and go as they please, so free to make a home away from home. Nowhere else are they so free to practice their religion, or express their sexuality, as they are in those nations Foucault decried as bastions of pastoral power.

The 'we' of the modern Nation State is neither exclusionary nor that which aims at racial or religious purity. It signifies a people bound not by blood or faith but by common fidelity to a given territory, its laws and institutions.[9] It signifies that 'we' belong to this particular place, one that 'we' love and consider as 'ours'. Naturally, people who belong to a given territory are bound by a shared past and a common language. This, however, does not serve as a barrier to those coming from elsewhere. In fact, the success of the American 'melting-pot model' rests on its insistence that newcomers claim that past and language as their own.

Of course, doing so requires much more than offering a verbal oath of loyalty to the Head of State or the constitution. It requires more than learning the basics of a language, as the problems of integrating certain immigrant communities in Europe suggest. Those problems notwithstanding, it is not a form of 'cultural violence' to insist that newcomers must strive to identify with the political order which has shaped the territory in which they are seeking to settle. For only by pledging their primary loyalty to the State and its institutions can they live in peace with those among whom they have come to make their new home. This does not mean that they must surrender their religious or 'cultural' practices, except in so far as those directly conflict with the law of the land. Notable examples of such practices are honour killings, forced female circumcision and forced marriages. Otherwise, the 'we' of the Western Nation State demands only that all citizens, regardless of origin, subscribe to a common set of laws and values enshrined in the constitution, and which define who 'we' are and what 'we' stand for. In that way, as Hegel puts it, identity is sustained amid difference, thus providing the conditions for a society to be at lasting peace with itself.

The important thing to note here is that, in those nations where such peace prevails, *the constitution is sovereign*. In states where the rule of man, or that of God, takes priority over that of law, there will either be tyranny or sectarian strife. That is because, where people are not subject to a common set of laws, they will offer their primary allegiance to sect, tribe or religion. This is what prompted an Irish Islamic leader to proclaim that, in the event of Muslims becoming a majority, Sharia or Holy Law would be imposed on Ireland. This is equivalent to the Catholic Primate of Ireland saying that, because Catholics are in a majority, Canon Law should be imposed across the land. The reason he would not say that is because yet another central feature of the Western political order is that both Church and State are equally subject to the requirements of the constitution. In other words, constitutional sovereignty safeguards against any single group seizing power against the will of the minority. It upholds an electoral process which ensures that all interests are represented. In so doing, it protects against those who would use elections to abolish elections, as happened recently in Egypt when the Muslim Brotherhood sought to undermine the constitution so as to maintain power in perpetuity. That is why when rulers seek to modify, amend or rewrite the constitution in their own favour, a country has taken its first steps along the road to serfdom.

For those who believe law is divinely sanctioned, the idea of a people being bound together through their common allegiance to the 'law of the land' is both alien and perverse. However, that is precisely how the people of the West traditionally organised their affairs. The Nation State was not an excuse for exclusion but that by which those who shared a common history consolidated their identity and preserved their ancestral settlement for those yet to come. Critics of the Nation State often claim there is nothing 'natural' about them, that they are contingent constructs whose origins were frequently marked by usurpation and violence. By and large that is true, and something few advocates of the Nation State would readily dispute. However, as Hegel reminds us, such things are 'matters for history' and do nothing to undermine the legitimacy of the State as it now stands. The important question for us is whether the State is prepared to deal with its past and to acknowledge those 'anonymous forces of history' who may not have always featured in its official history.

If Western nation states are prepared to do so, it is because they are, to repeat, *self-revising* entities. Like all nations, they have their myths of origin, but due to the liberty guaranteed under the law, those myths are subject to constant critique and revision. Only where the founding myth becomes immune to critique, where it assumes a quasi-religious status, will it be used as an excuse for exclusion and repression. This was the case in Nazi Germany and Soviet Russia, as it is currently in Cuba, North Korea and in the blood-soaked narratives of narrow nationalists like Sinn Fein.

As stated by Burke, 'it has been the uniform policy of our constitution to claim and assert our liberties, as an entailed inheritance derived to us from our forefathers, and to be transmitted to our posterity'. Consequently, our constitution 'preserves a unity in so great a diversity of its parts'.[10] The constitution and the institutions which sustain it reflect a long history of *homebuilding*. They serve as a record of negotiation and compromise, a testament to our ancestors' willingness to settle things through cooperation rather than force. In identifying with, and abiding by, the laws of the State as enshrined in the constitution, we 'are locked fast as in a sort of family settlement' – meaning that we respond with reverence to the sacrifices made on our behalf by the dead, while concurrently accepting the responsibility to transmit their legacy to the unborn.

The constitution is, thus, the perfect example of political and social ecology – a document which charts the evolution of the State and one which sustains the identity of the nation as reflected in its laws. It is 'living matter', in as much as it transmits 'our government and our privileges, in the same manner in which we enjoy and transmit our property and our lives'. Like any living organism, a political system held together by a constitution is a 'permanent body composed of transitory parts'; while the parts may change, the body itself remains in a 'condition of unchangeable constancy'. In showing how a people negotiated a common settlement, the document transmits to the living the wisdom of the dead. In reflecting the various changes in direction of the body politic, it contains within itself a history of our growth, one which provides the backdrop against which all future amendments and modification ought to take place. This is what Burke means when he writes that 'by preserving the method of nature in the conduct of the State, in what we improve, we are never wholly new; in what we retain we are never wholly obsolete'.[11] We are never 'wholly new' simply because, when we encounter a problem, we do not see that as an excuse to reject or abolish the prevailing constitutional structures. Rather, we modify the constitution so as to take account of the new difficulty. In other words, when the law fails to provide precedent, it must be improved to take account of changing circumstances. To improve something, however, does not make it obsolete. It simply enhances what is already there.

To perceive the State, its constitution and laws, as that which binds us to absent generations is to follow Burke in giving to 'our frame of polity the image of a relation of blood'. The law is not something alien or distinct from the individual, something which stands over and above him, but that in relation to which he establishes his true identity. In as much as we bind up 'the constitution of our country with our dearest domestic ties, adopting our fundamental laws into the bosom of our family affections', they become for us an object of loyalty and love. They attach us to this place we call 'home' and enable us to live in harmony with our neighbours. For even if we are not related by blood, we nevertheless share a common political and legal inheritance, a fact which allows us to recognise each other as *fellow citizens* – people for whom we may have to sacrifice our lives in any future emergency. We look on others, not as strangers or aliens, but as people united amid our differences and who share a common home. We are a people who can say 'we'.

Postmodernist lawyer Drucilla Cornell once declared that the law is 'a monster'. She did so because, as Caputo claims, the law 'is a calculated balance of payments, of crime and punishment, of offense and retribution, a closed circle of paying off and paying back'.[12] That is why the law requires what Caputo, following Derrida, calls 'justice', or that which prevents the law from shutting down or closing over. Justice is that which reminds the law that it can, and must, be revised in order to accommodate future difficulties and dilemmas. It is that which keeps the law (which is universal or applicable to all) sensitive to the singular situation or the individual case for which there is no precedent. The singular, Caputo writes, 'is what is always and already overlooked, out of sight, omitted, excluded, structurally, no matter what law, no matter what universal schema, is in place'.[13] Hence, when confronting an unforeseen case which cries out for justice, the law must be 'lifted or suspended, so that the judge "invents" the law for the first time, or, better, "re-invents" the law, not by beginning absolutely *de novo* but by making a "fresh judgment" … in a new situation. Such a decision, then, is both regulated (by law) and not regulated (responsive to justice), stretching the constraints of the law to include the demands of justice in a new, different, and singular situation.'[14]

The issue here is not whether Caputo and Derrida are right or wrong but whether their critique of the law in favour of justice ought to apply to the legal and judicial framework of Western nations, and especially to the tradition of common law. As defined by Caputo above, it seems to me that the 'deconstruction' of law is something integral to that framework and tradition. The common law is chiefly characterised by its openness to unforeseeable events and by its flexibility in relation to singular cases. We see this at work when the 'uncodified' or unwritten constitution of the United Kingdom is routinely amended on the basis of judicial reasoning in respect of unprecedented issues. Similarly, in those countries with a written constitution, we see it in operation when, in response to a moral or political crisis affecting the body politic, an issue is put to the people in the form of a constitutional referendum. In other words, the corrective of justice proposed by deconstruction to keep the law fair and flexible is presupposed by the very legal framework which Drucilla Cornell condemns as monstrous.

As I see it, laws are only monstrous when they cannot be adopted 'into the bosom of our family affections', when they pose a threat rather than a promise of peace and security. In those nations with a robust rule of law, where judicial independence is sacrosanct and where the 'method of nature' is preserved in the conduct of the State, citizens will not feel threatened but secure. However, when judicial independence is compromised, when the constitution is undermined or abolished, and when the law reflects only the interests of the governing elite, people will then cease to fully identify with it. It is then that they construe it as a 'monster' which must be obeyed, not out of love or loyalty but simply out of fear.

Once again, it is only in totalitarian or theocratic states that the idea of responding to the unique and singular case is anathema to the guardians of the law. If the law resists revision or emendation in such contexts, it is because it has become a tool in the armoury of the oppressor to vanquish opposition. Likewise, in deeming the law divine, the theocrat immunises it against interpretation or correction. As an eternal decree to which we must submit, it cannot be modified in response to what, from a celestial standpoint, are merely human needs or demands. Consequently, it stands in stark contrast to 'our' legal system which, for Burke, 'is placed in a just correspondence and symmetry with the order of the world'.[15]

In responding to the needs of their citizens, the constitutions and laws of Western states command respect and reverence. Like the rules of any household, they are seen not as a limitation on liberty but as that which ensures an equal measure of liberty for all. The spirit of freedom is, thus, 'tempered with an awful gravity'. Accordingly, ours is a 'noble freedom' which 'has a pedigree and illustrating ancestors'. Our laws are not rational abstractions that come from nowhere; neither did they fall readymade from the sky. They comprise a rich historical tapestry illustrating how 'we' came to be the people 'we' are. They show how, in response to unanticipated events, our ancestors reinterpreted the law so as to expand liberty beyond its previous bounds. The history of law is, therefore, the history of *our* liberty, an account of how it evolved on the basis of innumerable initiatives and compromises down the generations.

This helps explain why so many European citizens feel so detached and disconnected from the European Union. When legislation is ratified by national parliaments, it is, in most circumstances, willingly accepted by the subjects of those states. That is because they perceive it, not as a dictatorial ruling but as something written into law by people 'we' have voted into power and who 'we' can subject to scrutiny. Such politicians are limited by the constitution and, at the end of each parliamentary term, must give an account of themselves to their constituents. If they fail, they can be removed from office, either through disciplinary procedures or at election time. Their rulings have, accordingly, a human face, one to which citizens can apportion praise or blame.

The anonymous diktats which flow from the European Union have neither 'pedigree' nor 'illustrating ancestors'. They cannot be traced back to any particular politician who might then explain the reasoning behind them. Furthermore, they rarely respond to the particular problems faced by individual nation states, thus making them appear more like 'armed doctrine'. As incontestable impositions from nowhere, they cannot be readily applied to such states without simultaneously undermining the 'institutions of policy, the goods of fortune [and] the gifts of Providence' which 'are handed down, to us and from us, in the same course and order'.[16] That is because the rulings of the European Union are not based on local precedents which serve to guide judges and magistrates in the national context. Rather, they seem to be based on little more than the ideological preferences of their creators. In effect, this means their primary purpose is to impose change at the local level which corresponds to no pressing crisis or 'singular' situation on the ground. That is why European laws and regulations are now widely regarded – not only by conservatives but also by everyone except the most ardent Euro-enthusiasts – as deeply damaging to the social, political and legal fabric of individual nation states. They are rightly seen for what they are: an attempt to make us 'wholly new', thereby rendering wholly obsolete the noble idea that we should consider 'our liberties in the light of an inheritance'.

This is most obvious in the case of those rulings imposed on nation states by the European Court of Human Rights. As defined by both Burke and Hegel, a right is something which must be balanced against a *duty*. In recognising and undertaking my duties, I simultaneously recognise the extent of and limitations upon my rights. For Hegel, the State 'is the actuality of concrete freedom'. This means that it is only in and through participation in the State that the individual can enjoy true liberty. Only in recognising my obligations and responsibilities to others can I determine where personal freedom begins and where it ends. The law establishes those limits on my freedom, and, in upholding it, the individual acknowledges that 'in the State duty and right are united in one and the same relation'.[17]

There is, thus, an 'inter-penetration' of the universal and the particular, the State and the individual, right and responsibility. Unlike that purely abstract freedom proposed by Rousseau, Foucault and the new Jacobins – which is more like liberation from all constraint – concrete freedom implies a *certain degree* of constraint. It involves honouring one's obligations to the State, respecting private property and striving to fulfil the duties of citizenship. Such duties and responsibilities are not meant to deny freedom but to ensure the liberty of all so long as they live within the law. My rights are, thus, established by my duties and are only withheld when I contravene the law. Burke captured it well when he wrote that 'the restraints on men, as well as their liberties, are to be reckoned among their rights'.

There is, in other words, no abstract formula to determine what is or is not a right. Rights are the product of convention, of laws which emerge over time in response to particular problems in local contexts. In as much as the law of the land reflects the historical development of a particular people, it is a record of negotiation, compromise and consensus. It explains how and why 'we' manage our affairs as we do and also how we came to establish the limits of freedom and the extent of our civic duties. When observed in this way, rights are neither universal nor trans-historical but are rooted in the very soil of the State from which they have emerged.

In affirming another's rights, I am, therefore, recognising his freedom as permitted under a law to which we are both bound. In so doing, I acknowledge my duty to uphold his liberty so long as he honours his obligation to uphold mine. If we do so, it is not because the law is a monster or a menace which threatens our freedom but because we identify it as that without which no freedom worth its name could exist. The question then is this: how can any law-abiding citizen claim, 'under the conventions of civil society, rights which do not so much as presuppose its existence? Rights which are absolutely repugnant to it?'[18] Stated otherwise, how can 'we', as members of this particular society, claim rights which are at variance with the historical consensus as enshrined in our laws, the laws of *our* home?

The essential word in that question is 'claim'. For when rights are claimed in defiance of duty, it is an attempt to secure liberty on the cheap. It is an attempt to override the conventional consensus, regarding the nature and limits of rights, in my own favour. It is a demand that my right should come with no strings attached, that my claim should cost me nothing in terms of responsibility. In claiming freedom that is not shaped or constrained by convention, that does not presuppose the existence of a particular state, the individual disregards the concrete rights of his fellow citizens. In effect, he is saying that he is entitled to a greater share of freedom. It is a claim against the 'we' in respect of the 'I'.

That is why Burke took such exception to the *Declaration of the Rights of Man and the Citizen* (1789) which, in its doctrine of 'natural right', asserted that rights are universally valid throughout all times and places. Such rights may have the virtue of 'abstract perfection', but, in having no relationship to those rights and laws which are the 'offspring of convention', they are 'practically deficient'. While they may enter 'into common life like rays of light which pierce into a dense medium', such 'pretended rights' are, in reality, 'morally and politically false'. That is so because, unlike those rights founded on consensus, abstract rights are blind to those long-established compromises upheld by 'simple governments'. Hence they pose a direct risk to the delicate social balance sustained over generations by the 'constitution of a State, and the due distribution of its powers'.

Burke's critique was aimed at the 'converts of Rousseau' and the 'disciples of Voltaire', but it could equally apply to the

European Court of Human Rights. If its rulings are met with considerable resistance by the ordinary citizens of Europe, it is because they consider them as decrees which 'do not so much as suppose' the existence of the Nation State and are profoundly repugnant to it. If convention is the law of society, one that 'must limit and modify all the descriptions of constitution which are formed under it', it is without due regard to this law that European human rights rulings are made and imposed. This is especially so in the case of convicted criminals who appeal to the European Court on the basis that their 'human rights' have been infringed or of terrorists who fight against extradition to countries where, they claim, their human rights may be violated. By ruling in favour of such people, the European Court takes the side of the abstract over the concrete and practical. It ignores the fact that 'liberties and restrictions vary with times and circumstances' and 'cannot be settled upon any abstract rule'.[19] Most of all, however, it provides entitlements to those who, having failed in their duty to both the State and their fellow citizens, have willingly forfeited their freedom.

If this breeds resentment at the local or national level, it is because it undermines 'our' historic settlement. Giving freedoms to people without demanding any corresponding duties, or to those who have wantonly broken the law, is tantamount to ignoring the rights of those prepared to pay for their freedoms in duty and responsibility. The consequences of doing so are, however, anything but benign, as proven with the emergence of the prevailing 'rights culture'. The proliferation of rights at the expense of responsibility has only served to alienate people from each other, as they each vie to secure evermore 'inalienable' freedoms in the absence of social costs. Consequently, where rights were once rooted in a common fidelity to the law, thus binding citizens together, they are now the cause of significant division and disharmony. As American jurist Mary Ann Glendon explains, our 'rights talk, in its absoluteness, promotes unrealistic expectations, heightens social conflict, and inhibits dialogue that might otherwise lead towards consensus, accommodation, or at least the discovery of common ground'.[20] Quite simply, I would say it undercuts the law of the home.

Burke believed, quite correctly, that the constitution of a State, and the execution of its powers through civil institutions, is a 'matter of the most delicate and complicated skill'. That is so because, for a State to function, it must command the loyalty and affection of all its citizens. They must, that is, be capable of seeing in the State the principal source of their own happiness, security and fulfilment. This is what Hegel meant when he defined the State as 'the actuality of the ethical Idea'. It is only when the individual feels at home in the State, only when he conforms to its requirements and reaps the consequent benefits in terms of liberty, that this person will fully identify with the nation to which he belongs. The problem with the Jacobins, both old and new, is that by disregarding 'human nature and human necessities' in favour of pretended rights, they reduce 'the union of individuals in the State to a contract and therefore to something based on their arbitrary wills, their opinion'.[21] If the French Revolution did not usher in a new era of 'liberty, equality and fraternity', it was because its architects swept aside the constitution of a 'great actual state' for one that was based on 'pure thought alone'. The result, as correctly perceived by Hegel, was 'the maximum of frightfulness and terror'.[22]

If there is a salutary lesson here, it is that in the absence of nation states, people cannot identify with anything greater than themselves. They acknowledge a debt neither to the dead nor to the unborn and see the law as nothing more than a constraint on their arbitrary wills. Neither will they offer their allegiance to that which, as in the case of the European Union, seeks to supplant the nation as the principal object of their loyalty. The reason for this is that there is nothing in the European Union to which people feel fundamentally attached. Unlike the nation to which they are bound by history, language and culture, the federation is a contrived entity with which citizens cannot identify and which merely serves to alienate them from the political process. Having no roots in local soil, and issuing dictatorial directives from elsewhere, it simply cannot supply the rewards of membership which is the principal benefit of belonging to an actual state.[23] In losing their sense of ownership over the political process, people inevitably drift away from politics. When they no longer identify with the law of the home, or when they no longer recognise the home as *theirs*, it ceases to be an object of loyalty and affection. Proof of this can be seen in the widespread political apathy among younger voters across the European Union. If they have become detached and disinterested, it is because there is no place which they can readily identify as home, no place which the 'I' feels at one with the 'we'.

Conservatives are often accused of being enemies of the State and of promoting a form of radical individualism. Following the example of Margaret Thatcher, it is said, they wish to dismantle the State in favour of individual responsibility and that they see in unbridled capitalism the solution to every social and political dilemma. They are, thus, accused of fostering a culture of greed and selfishness and of offering ideological justification for so-called 'big business'. It is true that libertarians, and 'anarcho-capitalists' such as Murray Rothbard, consider the State as an impediment to liberty and regard the free market as a panacea to all social ills. However, it should be clear from what I have been arguing in this chapter that such ideas are more the exception than the norm among the founding fathers of philosophical conservatism.

When thinkers like Hegel and Burke speak of the State, it is certainly nothing akin to the socialist State which seeks to dominate the lives of its citizens. It comprises the institutional life a given territory, institutions (rule of law, independent judiciary and constitutional government) which guarantee liberty to engage in private pursuits within the constraints of the law. Naturally, within and between such states, there is free movement of goods and services. There is, in other words, a free market, one which is governed in accordance with the law of demand and supply. There is, however, nothing exploitative or unfair in this, being as it is the basis of a functioning *economy* (another meaning of *oikos-nomos* is the 'management of the home'). In the context of local economies, the free market is both protected and regulated by the institutional structures. That is, the law of the home ensures that the market remains both free and fair.

Global corporations which seek to exploit and thus destroy local economies find no favour among those for whom the State is, invoking Hegel again, the 'actuality of the ethical Idea'. That is why we can say, with Roger Scruton, that conservatism is less interested in profit than in loss. When defined as a form of political, cultural and moral *conservation*, the idea that conservatism is an enemy of the State, or an ally of big business, can no longer be sustained. Neither can it be accused of fostering a culture of selfishness in which the individual, unleashed from any attachment to the State, is considered sovereign. As I have described it here, conservatism is that which endeavours to sustain the State *against* its opponents, against those who would undermine the historical and political identity of its people and their common homeland. If anything promotes a culture of detached individualism, it is precisely those forces which, 'on the speculations of a contingent improvement', strive 'wholly to separate and tear asunder the bands of their subordinate community, and to dissolve it into an unsocial, uncivil, unconnected chaos of elementary principles'.[24]

If, to repeat, there is a political crisis affecting Europe, it is because people will always disconnect from that with which they cannot naturally identify. If their sense of belonging cannot be satisfied by a nebulous entity like the European Union, they will begin supporting political parties whose principal priority is to restore their historic settlement. The problem is, however, that the majority of those parties (National Front in France, UKIP in

Britain and Sinn Fein in Ireland) are disturbingly reactionary in nature. They are animated, not by a love of home, but by a narrow nationalism typified by the rigid ideology of 'ourselves alone' (a good translation of 'Sinn Fein'). To borrow Caputo's expression, their vision is of 'an airtight, impermeable, homogeneous, self-identical identity', as distinct from that more 'porous and heterogeneous' identity which characterises Western nations which are true to their political and cultural traditions.

If there is an answer to this, it is in that form of *patriotism* which is still actively promoted in the United States and which Hegel defined as 'assured conviction with truth as its basis'. Hegel believed that in the absence of robust institutions, such patriotism could neither flourish nor survive. Indeed, he went further and argued that action which does not conform to those institutions is *irrational*. As 'action in conformity with these institutions', patriotism derives from the 'consciousness' that my interest 'is contained and preserved' in the State. In what to my mind is still the finest definition of patriotism available, he wrote that while it is often understood 'to mean only a readiness for exceptional sacrifices and actions', it is however that sentiment which 'in the relationships of our daily life and under ordinary conditions, habitually recognises that the community is one's substantive groundwork and end'. And it is out of this consciousness, 'which during life's daily round stands the test in all circumstances, that there subsequently also arises the readiness for extraordinary exertions'.[25]

As used by Hegel, the word 'community' does not have the connotations of 'fusion' and 'identification' which Caputo attributes to conservatism. Following Derrida, Caputo writes that 'one must watch out for the ways tradition and community become excuses for conservatism, for the exclusion of the incoming of the other, and hence constitute "as much threat as promise," as much a trap as a tap'.[26] Conservatism, at least as I have defended it in this book, is a work not of exclusion but of love. That is why, when deployed by thinkers such as Hegel or Burke, community cannot be equated with 'a "common" (*com*) "defense" (*munis*), as when a wall is put up around the city to keep the stranger or the foreigner out'.[27] What they mean is precisely what Caputo means when he defines community as 'a common or shared life, from *com* + *munus*, having common "duties" or "functions," doing one's duty to the whole, mutual service'.[28]

As such, patriotism is that by way of which the individual identifies his interests and ends as coinciding with those of the community and his fellow citizens. It is that which enables him to see his destiny as intrinsically bound up with theirs and what motivates him, when summoned, to sacrifice on their behalf. However, patriotism is only possible where states and their institutions are strong and where, 'through the forming process of education', citizens act 'by reference to consciously adopted ends, known principles and laws'.[29] Those ends, principles and laws emerge over time and in response to concrete 'conditions and circumstances'. And if, as Burke put it, they do not leave us 'hesitating in the moment of decision' but rather engage 'the mind in a steady course of wisdom and virtue', it is because they are not the product of 'naked reason'. They derive, in large part, from those other 'integrating factors in the State' which implant a 'sense of unity in the depths of men's minds'.[30]

Such factors include our attachment to the land, to the cultural heritage of our shared home, and also to its religious rites and rituals. In each case, the individual is reminded that he belongs to something greater, something whose existence depends on the community for its survival. We are reminded that our obligations stretch much further than our rights and that, without all those who *cared for creation, conserved culture* and sought to *save the sacred* from desecration, we would have no freedom to speak of. For it is this – the pastoral, cultural and religious sentiments of a people – that renders a nation worthy of true love. It is this which offers redemption from alienation and which enables us to live lives of 'peace, and virtue, and fruitful penitence'.[31]

Notes

1   Burke, *Reflections*, p. 75.

2   John D. Caputo, *Deconstruction in a Nutshell* (New York: Fordham, 1997), p. 107.

3   Caputo, *Deconstruction in a Nutshell*, p. 106.

4   Michel Foucault, 'The Subject and Power', in Hubert L. Dreyfus and Paul Rabinow (eds), *Michel Foucault: Beyond Structuralism and Hermeneutics* (Chicago: Chicago University Press, 1982), p. 214.

5   Foucault, 'The Subject and Power', in Dreyfus and Rabinow (eds), *Michel Foucault: Beyond Structuralism and Hermeneutics*, p. 216.

6   Caputo, *Deconstruction in a Nutshell*, p. 122.

7   Caputo, *Deconstruction in a Nutshell*, p. 124.

8   Caputo, *Deconstruction in a Nutshell*, p. 113.

9   For more on the virtues of the nation, see Scruton, *The West and the Rest* (London: Continuum, 2003); *A Political Philosophy* (London: Continuum, 2006); and Section 2: 'The Nation', in Mark Dooley (ed.), *The Roger Scruton Reader* (London: Continuum, 2009). See also, Mark Dooley, *Roger Scruton: The Philosopher on Dover Beach* (London: Continuum, 2009), Ch. 5.

10   Burke, *Reflections*, p. 29.

11   Burke, *Reflections*, p. 29.

12   Caputo, *Deconstruction in a Nutshell*, p. 150.

13   Caputo, *Deconstruction in a Nutshell*, p. 135.

14   Caputo, *Deconstruction in a Nutshell*, pp. 136–7.

15   Burke, *Reflections,* p. 29.

16   Burke, *Reflections,* p. 29.

17   Hegel, *Philosophy of Right*, p. 161.

18   Burke, *Reflections*, p. 50.

19   Burke, *Reflections*, p. 51.

20   Mary Ann Glendon, *Rights Talk: The Impoverishment of Political Discourse* (New York: The Free Press, 1991), p. 14.

21   Hegel, *Philosophy of Right*, p. 157.

22   Hegel, *Philosophy of Right*, p. 157.

23   See Scruton, 'The Nation State and Democracy', in Dooley, *The Roger Scruton Reader*, pp. 75–87.

24   Burke, *Reflections*, p. 82.

25   Hegel, *Philosophy of Right*, p. 164.

26   Caputo, *Deconstruction in a Nutshell*, p. 109.

27   Caputo, *Deconstruction in a Nutshell*, p. 108.

28   Caputo, *Deconstruction in a Nutshell*, Note 4.

29   Hegel, *Philosophy of Right*, p. 165.

30   Hegel, *Philosophy of Right*, p. 168.

31   Burke, *Reflections*, p. 83.

7

Caring for creation

In our culture of immediacy, where the object of desire can be possessed with the click of a mouse, the time-honoured idea that we have a duty to care for creation is in danger of being lost. Believing that we can bypass the world and each other so as to instantly gratify our cravings, we have forgotten that we are ultimately dependent on others and the world for our survival. To recall the great lesson of Hegel's master–slave parable, no matter how self-sufficient the master believes he may be, he is ultimately reliant on another to sustain him in his mastery. The detached individual, who believes himself to be free of all social and natural constraints, is no less a creature of convention. He has been nurtured by a family, has been shaped by the norms and culture of his particular context, a fact which is obvious in everything he says and does. The liberal 'individual' is, thus, a product of the very past he seeks so desperately to deny. And, even when he claims to have outgrown his old self, it is only in contrast to it that he can establish a 'new' identity.

To say, in other words, that you are opposed to something is to affirm the very thing you are against. In Hegelian terms, the master's entire identity is intrinsically bound up with that of the slave. He may deny his servant, but he is only master by virtue of his relationship to the slave. Hence, notwithstanding his claims of liberty and independence, the master is fundamentally defined by his relationship to the slave. That is why Hegel believed it is irrational to seek to live as though you were not part of a greater whole – part of a state, society and community which precedes and which forms the so-called 'individual'. It is irrational because the result of such experiments in living is, as I have been arguing throughout this book, alienation and estrangement from those forms of life which render existence meaningful. However, it is both natural and rational to want to belong to a place you can call 'home'. It is true that, in so doing, we acknowledge our reliance on others, but, unlike that of the master, this is not a form of dependency which equates to addiction. Rather, it is simply to recognise that each person is in debt to parents, family, society and creation itself, for the liberties they now enjoy.

In the words of moral philosopher Alasdair Macintyre, we are 'dependent rational animals'.[1] From the moment of birth, we rely on others to care for and protect us from danger and harm. At both ends of life, when we are most helpless, we depend on people to sacrifice on our behalf. That is why, to recall what I said in a previous chapter, the habit of sacrifice is so vital to the maintenance of society. Without sacrifice, the treasures of the dead will neither be preserved nor transmitted to the living. People will refuse to forgo the pleasures of immediacy for the long-term security of helpless others. We see this currently at work in the breakdown of family life, rapidly declining birth rates and a general loss of respect for the elderly. In a society that lives only for itself, one that has forgotten whence it came, the very young and the very old are considered a burden too heavy to shoulder. Yet, the fact remains that we owe our very existence to the old. Without their sacrifice, we would not be in possession of the freedoms we claim as our own. Similarly, when a society ceases to produce children, it is a sign that it is no longer prepared to surrender for absent others. It is an indication of our refusal to extend to future generations the chances which we ourselves have been afforded.

This explains why conservatives place such weight on the concept of *husbandry*. In its traditional sense, the husband was 'master of the home', a prudent or frugal manager of scarce resources. He was an 'economist', a homebuilder whose task it was to domesticate the world in order to provide an enduring settlement for his family. As such, the husband was responsible for *caring*, *conserving* and *cultivating*. He was both *father* and *farmer*, someone who sought to adapt a given territory to the needs of his dependents. Today, husbandry is solely synonymous with farming, but it is important to retain both senses of the word. That is because parenting is no less a form of husbandry than farming. In creating and caring for their children, parents ensure the conservation of memory, wisdom and virtue. In making a home, one in which children are educated and cultivated culturally, they serve to link the generations through bonds of affection and love. And it is in this, the husbanding of social and spiritual resources, that parents fulfil their true role as conservationists.

Good parenting means not only caring for a child's body but also caring for and nourishing his soul. As I suggested in Chapter 2, it means shaping him in accordance with the objective norms and values of society. It means teaching him that all rights must be paid for from the bank of responsibility. Such is the process of civilising and forming children as *citizens* or as those who identify with a given place and who adopt its fundamental laws into the bosom of their family affections. It is, thus, the process of building a solid identity that enables children to feel at ease in their world. Of course, parents are not obliged to pass down those resources which are the fruits of much sacrifice. As is so often the case, they can simply ignore their children's 'spiritual' requirements, responding only to their basic physical needs. The result, I have suggested, is that children remain as aliens to themselves and to the surrounding society. If this is the root cause of much 'antisocial behaviour', it is because estrangement breeds resentment. When children do not feel at home, they end up at war with those who do. Without the spiritual security which firmly roots them in a place shaped by the sacrifices of their predecessors, they will never acquire that secure sense of self which will, in turn, prompt them to sacrifice for those yet to come.

As I have discovered in my own life as both husband and father, children long to belong. They long to identify with something greater than the isolated self, to something that will supply them with lasting sense and meaning. When considered as husbandry, as an essential form of caring for creation, the role of parents is to integrate their children into those institutions where those longings will be fulfilled. That is, children are completely dependent on their parents to shape their identity and to transmit to them the resources which constitute the good or virtuous life. I saw this vividly when, after attending Mass in the ancient Latin rite of the Roman Catholic Church, my eldest son asked if he could serve there as an altar boy. Despite the fact that he was only six years of age, he still sensed that this was no ordinary ritual. Through the sacred sounds of Palestrina and Byrd, in the haunting Latin chants and in a ceremony characterised by grace, beauty and harmony, one little boy caught a glimpse of paradise.

However, he was also drawn by the voice of tradition that called from the very depths of this sacramental experience. He wanted to know *why* the priest faced the tabernacle rather than the people, *why* the Mass was structured so differently to the 'vernacular' and *why* the ritual was characterised by such aesthetic splendour. In explaining all this to my son, and in subsequently allowing him to become an altar boy, I was not only answering to his religious requirements but signing him up to 'the great primeval contract of eternal society'. In a very real way, this would help conserve and sustain a form of life steeped in convention, culture and the religious rites of his ancestors. In answering to so many of his needs on so many levels, my son's serving at the altar has confirmed me in my conviction that the best way parents can care for their creation is to husband those resources which are vital for virtue, and without which no child can realise his or her full potential.

Parents, to repeat, *domesticate* the world for their children. In so doing, they seek to make it familiar and lovable, to render it peaceful and secure. The family home provides the context in which the world is tamed, where it becomes an object less threatening than enchanting and consoling. To build a home means to fence off a given plot of land, to place it on solid foundations and to shape it in the image of its proprietors. It is to see in the soil not only a place of refuge and rest but also a settlement where 'we' have put down roots. It is a symbol of our desire to survive beyond the fleeting moment. I have argued that in the liberal world, in Cyberia, people rarely put down roots. Hence they are disconnected from their past, from each other and from the earth. Conversely, in planting roots, we follow Burke in 'preserving the method of nature in the conduct of the state'. We connect with the real world, with real people and, in so doing, establish an embedded identity.

There is much that we have lost in the way of pastoral wisdom. We have taken flight from the land and, thus, from the ancient homestead of the heart. However, even urban dwellers can still recreate something of that experience through *gardening*. Philosophers rarely discuss gardening, and yet it is an activity with deep philosophical significance.[2] In a world so threatened by ecological degradation – spiritual, cultural and environmental – the garden represents for many their last link to the land and to the wisdom of absent generations. For it is through gardening that we root ourselves to the soil, that we learn how to respond to the demands of nature and to respect those creatures with whom we share this earth. It is to learn to live by the seasons and to engage with the world in a way that is conducive to both health and harmony. Through gardening, we overcome the modern disease of *displacement*. In planting, cultivating, sowing and weeding, gardeners spread themselves across nature. They work the soil in the manner of Hegel's slave, imbuing it with a sense of their own identity. In so doing, they claim ownership over a particular place, suggesting to all who pass that this is where 'we' belong.

To garden is to put down roots. It is to cultivate a small plot of earth to the point where it mirrors its owners' desire to dwell and, indeed, their aesthetic preferences. Hence, our gardens convey a sense of who 'we' are and what we value. A carefully crafted garden, one in which shrubs and plants are tenderly maintained, reflects its owners' pride in that place. It reveals the importance in their lives of beauty and order, of maintaining a place which is not just a plot or a house but a home. In as much as they disclose how we wish to be perceived, our gardens are a window to the soul. They indicate where we stand, not only in relation to the environment but also to the rest of the community. For when I resolve to tackle the garden, I do so with the aim of fitting in with my general surrounds. I do so because a beautiful garden signifies its owner's intention to contribute to the aesthetic order of the street. It indicates my longing to harmonise with my neighbours. Consider, for example, how a garden can bind strangers in a web of mutual dependence. Think of the leisurely conversations across the hedge, the various tips exchanged and the invitations offered. Think of how, through pruning and planting, we come to appreciate just how symbiotically attached we are to those on the other side. In and through gardening, the individual lives the 'life of the whole' in himself.

For children, the importance of gardening cannot be overestimated. In Cyberia, they are attached to nothing and nowhere. However, in the garden they are firmly rooted. They are bound to the earth, to life and to a concrete community. My children never thrive more than when elbow-deep in muck. Indeed, everything they know about the natural world, and their place in it, derives from their time spent among the shrubs. It is there that they have experienced nature as a source of wonder, beauty and sustenance. It has taught them to see beyond the screen into a world from which we cannot totally detach. Contrary to the illusions of mastery conjured in Cyberia, it has taught them that we are, of necessity, reliant on that which we so often endeavour to ignore. As such, it has given them a sense of the interconnectedness of life, of their place in the broader scheme of things. In observing worms and spiders, bees and birds, my sons have come to appreciate why these species are important to the fragile ecosystem and why our fate is so inextricably bound up with theirs. Without the experience of gardening, in which they abide in the midst of creation, the children of Cyberia cannot really understand why protecting the environment is a moral necessity.

This vital experience is, of course, amplified in farming – a form of life rapidly disappearing from our world but one no less fundamental to our survival. Indeed, for detached city dwellers, the farm is now more a quaint curiosity than a place where we can feel truly at home. As it happens, my wife passed much of her childhood on her father's farm in Ireland, and it is to this rural idyll that we migrate for a period each summer. In so doing, we have come to realise that the transition from city to country life represents not only a change of location but a radical alteration in the way we experience the world. If the city is animated by noise and mayhem, the country is a place of peace. If the city never sleeps, the country is a place where life is still governed by the gentle rhythms of the natural order.

As we leave behind the sirens and smog, the gridlock and the gadgets, we enter a pastoral oasis where that old order still obtains. There are trees here which date back centuries, and whose enormous branches provide natural shade against the late summer sun. Standing beneath them, you are reminded just how provisional human life is and how much it owes to the land. That is also true of the animals that dwell here. No less than the trees and hedgerows, the horses and cattle are at one with the soil, it being the source of life itself. From the moment we arrive on the farm, we too become rooted. We awake not to the sound of a clock but to the whispers of those great trees as they sway in the morning breeze. It is as if they are summoning us to rise with the sun and to sanctify the hours in pastoral tranquillity.

For farm folk, conservation is not so much a duty as a way of life. As people rooted to the land, theirs is an existence which preserves intact the practical wisdom of the dead, thus ensuring its transmission to the unborn. That is why, in so many ways, the farm provides a marvellous moral education, one that prioritises love of land, family and settlement. It teaches the value of roots to a world where there are none. At a time when children are so disengaged from such vital things, it is a powerful reminder that, as creatures of the earth, we cannot thrive when stuck to a screen. Such is what Heidegger called 'dwelling'. In the cities of Cyberia, people exist but they no longer dwell. That is because dwelling cannot be hurried, dedicated as it is to homemaking, building and belonging. The farm stands as a glorious testament to those old virtues. It is a form of life in which family still matters, and in which man's primal relationship to the earth is still valued and sustained. It is there that people can rediscover how to dwell in a place whose roots are still strong.

Living alongside animals teaches what was obvious to our ancestors but is now routinely dismissed by liberals. It reminds us that we belong to an order structured by a rigid hierarchy. The fact that humans rank above animals in that hierarchy puts paid to the notion that little separates the species. The school curriculum teaches my children that certain countryside pursuits are a violation of 'animal rights'. On the farm, they quickly learn that animals do not have rights, simply because, as Scruton so often writes, nonhuman creatures cannot be held morally accountable for their actions.[3] My boys soon learn why it is an absurdity to claim that 'animal liberation' should be the principal goal of all conscientious people. This, of course, does not mean that farmers do not love their animals but only that they love them *as* animals, not as quasi-humans.

In tending to their creatures, farmers rely upon tried and trusted techniques handed down through the generations. They endure only because they listen to the land, carefully observe the lessons of nature and rarely deviate from the common sense of their ancestors. It takes effort to rise with the sun in order to feed the animals each day of the year. It takes effort to maintain a farm in an age so sceptical of that ancient way of life and to uphold the old virtues of rural life such as caring for family, neighbours and for creation itself. Those who make that effort are, however, rewarded in knowing that they are preserving something precious from extinction.

Farming is not an easy life by any standards, and those who persist are, in many cases, very close to giving up. If that is tragedy for the farmer himself, it is no less so for society in general. For with every farm that disappears, we lose a little more of that vital knowledge which all societies require in times of necessity. Farming teaches us self-reliance, something which, as we shall see below, is also true of the garden vegetable-patch. It provides us with the know-how to adapt the environment to our needs, especially when times are tough. That is why it is sheer folly to look upon its current difficulties with indifference, for it is a mistake to take anything for granted, most especially our food supply. Unless, therefore, we provide incentives for young farmers to stay rooted, we may very soon find ourselves struggling to endure.

My children are lucky to have access to those pastoral treasures denied to so many. As they wander around the farm in their little boots, their hands and faces thick with grime, I think of all we stand to lose should the present trend against farming continue. I think not only of the practical damage but also of the moral consequences this will pose for their descendants. For it is here on farms like this, that the timeless moral sense still chimes.

It is here, where time has little purchase, that family life still flourishes and the relaxed routines of a gentler age prevail. It is here, where the earth is soaked in memory, and where the whispering trees sing to the spirit, that the heart of a country continues to beat. My time spent on the farm has taught me the truth of something so often denied by the denizens of nowhere: agricultural life is not a burden but a benediction, one which draws us back to the soil, and thus to the ancestral homeland of the soul.

Roots are difficult to put down but easy to sever. Precious things that have been built up over generations take but a wet day to destroy. And the most effective way to destroy them is through simple neglect. If farmers resist the culture of amnesia, it is because they simply cannot afford to forget. With Burke, they cherish all their old 'prejudices', by which he did not mean narrow-minded bigotry but all those customs and conventions which have lasted because they have been found to work. As such, those wedded to the soil do not 'live and trade each on his own private stock of reason' but readily 'avail themselves of the general bank and capital of nations and of ages'. In learning from the land, their animals, and in preserving the wisdom and virtue of their predecessors, they are not left 'hesitating in the moment of decision, sceptical, puzzled, and unresolved'. Rather, their virtue becomes their habit; their duty becomes a part of their nature.

This, of course, is not to argue that people should migrate from Cyberia back to the farm. We have fled from the soil and there is, alas, no returning. That acknowledged, people can still choose, even when living in the heart of a city, to live like farmers. We can always adapt their wisdom and way of life to our own. To do so would involve factoring the earth back into our daily dealings. It would be to see it, not solely as a resource for our use or abuse but as a gift from the dead to the unborn. It would be to see it as something which has been shaped and moulded by our ancestors, something which contains their consciousness and thus something which we are duty-bound to sustain. Sustainability and husbandry are, thus, the priorities for those who see the necessity of reconnecting to the earth. And if they are to become our habit or part of our nature, we must endeavour to exist in the constant awareness that caring for creation is a precondition for lasting happiness.

I have already suggested that one of the ways for urban dwellers to reconnect with the earth is through gardening. The garden is a microcosm of the farm, a place where children can observe the natural order at close quarters. It teaches them how to sustain and respect the multifarious forms of life which are simply ignored in Cyberia, but which are no less vital for survival and sustainability. It also conserves those practical techniques which have been transmitted down the generations, the application of which 'engages the mind in a steady course of wisdom and virtue'. This is especially so in those gardens where vegetables are sown and grown.

If there is a way to inspire reverence for creation in children, it is by permitting them to take responsibility for a small vegetable plot. In learning how to sow seeds, and in tending to them daily, children not only witness the miracle of natural growth, which, of course, is an education in itself. They also learn how to sustain and husband resources from plot to plate. In seeing their toil bear fruit, they begin to recognise how interdependent we are with the land. Like Hegel's slave, they begin to see their lives endorsed by the earth, to see in the soil a reflection of the self. It is as if, along with the vegetables, their identity takes root. In a very tangible way they are attaching themselves, not merely to the earth but also to their ancestry. To perceive the soil as soaked in memory, to relate to it as the root source of identity, ensures that everything undertaken in the garden is transformed into a work of love.

In bringing their vegetables to fruition, children also learn how to conquer the illusions of mastery engendered by postmodern life. When the time arrives to pick and consume the product of their labour, they realise that food cannot be manufactured from nowhere. They realise that consumers are dependent on producers who are, in turn, dependent on creation. If this is vital knowledge, it is because it prevents children from taking for granted what they possess or consume. For they now know that however convenient it might be to deny our dependency on others and the earth, we are, nevertheless, inextricably bound to both. In taking pride in their produce, they recognise that when we treat the soil with respect, it will offer up a bountiful harvest. As such, a deep connection is forged with the land, one that will never be broken and that will serve to keep them scrupulously aware of how vital creation is to our survival.

Wherever things are grown, in however small a quantity, the virtues of husbandry and conservation become the norm. Like farmers, we begin to take notice of the soil and to recognise that all things have their due season. We also reacquire the habit of sacrifice, moderation and patience. That is because, in tending to the earth, our eyes are not solely fixed on the present but also on both the past and the future. In allowing the earth to shape the way we live, we emulate the example of our ancestors – those for whom the land was a source of sustenance, their livelihood and a bequest to those yet to come. We come to terms with the fact that environmental degradation is neither cost-free nor morally neutral. It is, rather, nothing less than a squandering of inherited resources without any regard for those whose world this will one day become. It is to believe that we are somehow entitled to plunder the gifts of creation for our benefit alone, to pillage what we ought to sustain for the sake of our successors. Realising the consequences for our descendants of waste, we thus begin to live as the land demands. We begin to temper our desires, moderate our impulses and exist in the conscious awareness that the earth is not inexhaustible.

To acquire this pastoral perspective means altering the way *we* live, travel and eat. It is also to give due consideration to where you purchase goods and products. The world of the master is one of convenience, where every luxury is obtained on demand and in ignorance of its origin. That we are all masters now only proves that we, too, no longer care how our goods are produced or by whom. This has been exacerbated by the phenomenon of 'online shopping', a process which is steadily wiping out the local shop and market. To purchase from a shop or market involves much more than selecting produce of the finest quality, and which could be sourced back to a local supplier. Fundamentally, it is a social experience in which the shopper directly engages with shopkeepers and traders, friends and neighbours. Shopping provides people with a rich sense of social solidarity, a sense that their visit to the village is less out of mere necessity but more from a desire to connect with those who share a common homestead.

Online shopping destroys that valuable social experience because the purchaser seeks refuge behind a screen. In connecting to an online shop, he disconnects not only from his neighbours but also from all those who, in the case of food, deliver it from plot to plate. As such, the purchaser becomes dislocated from the earth and all those who tend to it. That is why, in mediating with the world through a screen, we are less likely to acquire the pastoral perspective, less liable to sacrifice for those who are brought into view through direct contact with creation. When, however, we take time to grow what we can, and to purchase the remainder from local shopkeepers and traders, we reconnect with our place, its people and its past. We resist the lure of convenience for a sustainable life, one in which our immediate needs are always measured against those of our progeny. This means following seriously the great insight of St Teresa of Avila that 'patient endurance attaineth to all things', especially in our relationship to food.

Consuming food is, quite literally, a process of becoming one with the earth.[4] It involves taking what is alien and other and making it part of oneself. Hegel called this the 'identity of identity and non-identity', by which he meant a union of sameness (me) and otherness (the world). It is to ingest the world, or, to borrow the religious vernacular, to *commune* with it. Through eating, we commune with creation: I 'take in' or consume what was once foreign and different, thereby making it part of me. However, this process involves much more than simply devouring whatever the eye desires. If the raw food in the ground or on the shelf is neither immediately desirable nor appetising, it is because it must first be transformed into something with which I can identify. Hence the importance of the culinary arts, those techniques by which the world is made edible.

Through cooking, what was once alien becomes desirable, what was once different becomes familiar. Cooking does not solely involve destroying bacteria harmful to humans. It involves imbuing food with the values of the household. There is, in other words, a cultural and aesthetic dimension to cooking which infuses the raw material with a spiritual significance. By this, I mean that when food is prepared according to conventional techniques, it acquires an almost human face. Even before it enters the oven, it is something we can admire and relish. No longer is it raw, and thus an alien entity with which we cannot identify, but something which we have made our own. And if we savour the prospect of consuming it, it is because the food has been transformed into our image and likeness. We see it as a source of satisfaction because, through labour, it has acquired an attractiveness which, in its raw state, it simply did not possess.

As a process through which we mediate with the world, conventional cooking involves delayed gratification. It involves work and time, dedication and commitment. If that is so, it is because a meal is not merely a means of nourishing the body but also of replenishing the spirit. Not only does the meal bind us to creation, but it also binds us to each other. The meal is that which gathers us together and which serves to sanctify our common sense of belonging. It reminds us that we belong to the earth, that it is the source of our sustenance and the wellspring of this place we call home. In sharing a meal, we express our reliance on the earth, but we also affirm our reliance on those who sit by our side. In breaking bread together, we become one with family and friends. As such, the host provides the context in which the sharing of food and wine serves as a symbolic endorsement of our settlement.

That the same cannot be said for fast food is, I have argued, because it serves merely to fill an intestinal hole rather than a spiritual void. Once again, the object is immediate gratification rather than delayed satisfaction. However, without the labour involved in slow cooking, we lose sight of food as a product of the earth. No longer is it considered something of intrinsic worth, something which binds and ties, but rather that which we consume out of mere necessity. It is then that eating becomes a purely functional exercise devoid of its ceremonial dimension. Emptied of its social and aesthetic element, food no longer serves as a source of belonging but only of isolation, estrangement and disconnection. When consumed on the hoof and from a box, it is drained of its communal significance and thus of its power to unite.

In like manner, the so-called 'TV dinner', even if consumed in company, bears no relation to the traditional meal. Mass-produced and requiring no preparation or cooking, it is the perfect sustenance for the culture of amnesia – a culture that has forgotten its reliance on the earth. In so many ways, what we consume, and the way in which we do so, defines the type of people we are. It says what we value and how we relate to creation. That is why the distinction between the family meal and the TV dinner is not just a difference in taste. It is the difference between food considered as a source of physical, social and moral nourishment and that which we eat merely to satisfy the stomach and fend off exhaustion. Hence, those who eat traditionally are more likely to care both for creation and for community. They are more likely to see through the illusions of mastery and to respect our reliance on others and the gifts of the earth. By eschewing solitary for communal satisfaction, they opt for the 'we' over the 'I'.

If fast food encourages binge eating, slow food forces us to temper our appetites. It encourages moderation and balance in a society where excess is now the norm. It promotes denial and sacrifice over indulgence and gluttony. For Aristotle, human flourishing required acting in accordance with virtue, where virtue was defined as a mean between the two extremes of excess and deficiency. If there is no virtue in extremism, it is because it signifies an unhealthy relationship with reality. There is, in other words, a virtuous way of relating to the earth, one tangible benefit of which is health in mind and body. To feed the appetites without restraint is, therefore, to deny virtue in favour of vice. This is no less true when appetite is repressed in favour of rigid restraint.

Slow food discourages both these extremes by cultivating virtue. In sharing a drink prior to the meal, we bring a sense of ceremony to the occasion. Conversation encourages sipping rather than gulping, savouring rather than swigging. The aperitif is the perfect prelude to that shared experience of ingesting the world and celebrating it as that to which we belong. It signifies that our relationship to the earth is much more than one of necessity; it reminds us of our common destiny and our will to survive against all the odds. It also suggests that when eating and drinking are taken out of their communal context, they risk being emptied of virtue. For it is the presence of others which serves to prevent the isolation which is characteristic of excess and deficiency.

In disposing of the culinary arts, and the spiritual nourishment they supply, we stand in danger of severing our bonds to a more generous, graceful and virtuous world. That is a world in which selfishness is the exception and hospitality the norm, one in which the meal represents an occasion not for excess but for sharing and caring. It is a world where elegance surrounds the process of eating and where ceremonial effort is rewarded with blessed memories and lasting love. In contrast to TV dinners and convenience food, which foster alienation and detachment, the family meal celebrates and reinforces our togetherness. Although neglected, this is, however, something which can always be revived. It does not take much to set a table each evening, pour a tincture of wine, light a candle and feast, however modestly, with one's family. The cost of not doing so is nothing less than losing a sense of the land and of our place in it.

Those most vocal in their support of the environment are, ironically, the children of Cyberia and liberals who have long since rejected the idea of home. However, as Scruton rightly suggests, you can only truly care for what you know and for what is buried deep in your natural affections.[5] This means that people are wrong to think about the environment in global rather than local terms. At its most effective, caring for creation involves living one's daily life with a pastoral outlook. It requires never losing sight of the earth and never ceasing to responsibly husband resources in whatever small ways we can. Domesticating the planet is something we humans must do to survive. Hence it is of no value to demand that we simply detach from the earth and dwell nowhere. Far better, it seems to me, that we affirm our right to dwell in this place that is ours, dutifully conserving it for future generations, while never ceasing to ensure that those who belong here remain firmly rooted to the soil.

Notes

1 See Alasdair Macintyre, *Dependent Rational Animals: Why Human Beings Need the Virtues* (Chicago: Open Court, 1999).

2 The exceptions are David E. Cooper, *A Philosophy of Gardens* (Oxford: Oxford University Press, 2006) and Scruton, *Beauty* (Oxford: Oxford University Press, 2009), pp. 80–2.

3 See Scruton, *Animal Rights and Wrongs* (London: Continuum, 2000).

4 See the beautiful book by Leon Kass, *The Hungry Soul: Eating and the Perfecting of Our Nature* (Chicago: The University of Chicago Press, 1994).

5 See Scruton, *Green Philosophy* (London: Atlantic Books, 2012).

8

Conserving culture

Philosophers, art historians, anthropologists, sociologists and literary critics have produced many different definitions of culture, ranging broadly from the cultivation of the mind to the exaltation of a nation's *Geist*, to a wide array of expressions of identity. I suggest that those three understandings can be reconciled by seeing culture as homebuilding. Like the process of homebuilding, the work of culture is that whereby we settle in a place and shape it in our own image. Derrida said as much when he wrote that the 'movement of culture' involves *domestication*, or making something 'part of the household'.[1] Through culture, we render the world recognisable as 'ours'. We mark and mould the land so that it becomes a place where the self can feel at home, a place that endorses the identity of those dwelling there. In the process, the earth assumes a human form, one that mirrors the ideals, values and norms of its inhabitants. This is expressed not only in the dominant architectural style of a given place but also in its symbols, flags and emblems. Those objects signify what 'we' stand for, how 'we' live and what 'we' value. They signify the law of the home (*oikos-nomos*). The work of culture is, thus, a work of domestication in which we imprint on the world our sense of self.

A country's culture tells us everything about the way its citizens live, their habits and their political, moral and social customs. We distinguish the English from the French, for example, on the basis of culture and style. From architecture to clothing, and from food to literature, we observe distinctions which indicate how they view themselves and their relationship to the wider world. When we compare French and English cuisine and norms of hospitality, we are, in effect, contrasting sacramental and functional ways of relating to the earth, to the table and to the guests around it. For, to repeat, how and what people eat suggests how they care for creation. As with the home, we can see from the way it is designed and decorated what its owners cherish and esteem. From the way their property is planned, we can tell much about how they relate to the environment and to each other. Their civic buildings will reveal where they stand politically, while a nation's public monuments speak of its history and what it continues to value despite the passage of time.

Endowing all stages of homemaking with significance, culture can also be said to constitute a work of memory, mourning and love. In as much as the present generation retains and conserves its cultural inheritance, it keeps alive the memory of all those who domesticated a particular place. It honours those who, through the work of culture, shaped and sanctified the soil. It commemorates absent generations, not only through formal rites and rituals which invoke the dead but through those everyday practices which sustain the law of the home. Conserving culture is an act of love for a way of life we owe to others, and which depends on us for its continuation. It is a way of identifying with our deceased and of honouring their sacrifices.

That is why, in teaching children how to dress and speak in accordance with convention, in teaching them what is right to revere and respect, we are teaching them nothing less than how to belong. We are giving them a concrete sense of identity formed over generations and preserved in stone, cloth and ceremony. In disposing of culture, therefore, we are not merely disposing of some antiquated wisdom whose time has come and gone. To recall what I said regarding architecture in Chapter 4, when we cease to build, dress and eat in line with established norms, we cease to dwell in the shadow of 'canonised forefathers'. We sever our ties to the past, to the insights of our dead and thus to our spiritual homestead.

Liberalism involves the assumption that, because cultural differences are 'artificial', they can easily be swept away. However, as the postmodern politics of the European Union clearly demonstrates, there is much more at stake than simply substituting one flag for another. In reshaping the cultural contours of a country to reflect a new political reality, in reconfiguring its architecture, symbols, and even its currency, you radically change the way it relates to its past, its neighbours and the wider world. Not only do you undermine traditional loyalties, but you also alter the self-perception of a people to the point where they no longer recognise whence they came. It is to demolish a concrete cultural patrimony which commands affection and fidelity in favour of a culture of amnesia which binds people to nothing and nowhere.

This is obvious in the flag, insignia and architecture of the European Union, all of which symbolise detachment over domesticity, alienation over identity. Whereas the flag and civic buildings of each member state bear witness to its unique cultural identity, history and political values, those of the European Union are inventions *ex nihilo*. Only a culture which connects people to their dead, only one which gives them a sense of home and belonging, can command lasting loyalty and devotion. Being devoid of such culture, the European Union is, as I have suggested, more a product of 'naked reason' than of practical wisdom or virtue.

It is the fact that culture gathers, binds, houses and connects, which makes it an object of suspicion and critique for those who seek to cut the chains of convention. When Derrida describes culture as the work of domestication, he does so with a view to illustrating what it *cannot* contain or house. To return to the argument of previous chapters, deconstruction emphasises loss, forgetfulness and absence, over memory, renewal and presence. It insists that all identity is porous and essentially hollow at its core. From this perspective, culture is always already detached from its original or founding event. What it seeks to commemorate has already been erased by time, leaving only a trace in its wake. It is, therefore, a 'treasury of traces' open to endless reinterpretation and revision and not something which serves to invoke the *presence* of the dead.

If culture is memorialisation, or an attempt to house the spirit of the dead among the living, Derrida believes that this attempt will always fall short. For what we are dealing with in culture is simply the 'remains' of events, of people and their work. By its very nature, repetition divorces us from the original experience of something. It pushes us further away from the founding event and thus from its true significance and meaning. For Derrida, the reality of loss becomes apparent when 'I know that things don't repeat and that the repetition I love is not possible; this is what I call loss of memory, the loss of repetition, not repetition in the mechanical sense of the term, but of resurrection, resuscitation, regeneration.'[2]

In order to further illustrate this point, Derrida cites the examples of 'laughter, song and tears', none of which can be inscribed and, consequently, transmitted or captured in stone, in print or on canvas. They represent a 'non-repeatable singularity', meaning that they cannot survive 'the singular and unique moment of [their] apparition'. Laughing, crying and singing constitute a very particular response to very singular situations, situations which cannot be repeated. We cannot 'send tears through the mail', nor can we send 'a burst of laughter or a song'. If that is true of the postal service, it is equally so of cultural transmission. In seeking to hand on our cultural heritage, we attempt, as it were, to mail it to the next generation. In so doing, however, we put even more distance between us and what we are seeking to resuscitate. The original event is further effaced in the process of trying to keep it alive. According to Derrida, this is because, with time and repetition, we simply lose sight of the origin. Like a family keepsake that is handed down from one generation to the next, it becomes worn and faded until such time as it loses all relevance and meaning. If culture cannot ultimately contain or keep things intact, if it fails in its attempt to domesticate and retain the past, it is because integral to this process is loss.

Derrida was always at pains to say that his work was not primarily concerned with loss but was a positive affirmation of what cannot be resurrected. As he wrote, '[W]hat pains me, over and above all the other possible kinds of suffering, is the fact that things get lost.'[3] Deconstruction was, for him, a mode of interpreting culture which, while acknowledging that memory is somewhat 'bereaved', persists in affirming what it knows to be irretrievably lost or forgotten. However, the point of the exercise was not to *conserve* culture as something constitutive of identity but to demonstrate how identity is unsettled by that which can never be made present. It was to prove that, because the work of culture is fundamentally undermined by its inherent failure to retain the uniqueness of past events, we are basically rootless and without a proper home. It was to show that there can be no mastery of memory, in the sense that all writing or inscription – all culture – can never fully re-create or resurrect the original order of things. However hard we try to sustain the law of the home through symbols, literature, painting, music, or even through our everyday cultural norms, we are inevitably led to the realisation that what we believe they conserve simply cannot be kept.

Derrida sought to illustrate this by writing 'books' which were not really books. For him, to write a book in the conventional mode is an attempt to contain, control and gather. The cover of a book is analogous to a border, margin or perimeter which secures the text's identity. It is an attempt to prevent loss, to stop anything from escaping beyond 'border control'. This is especially so in the case of a biography or autobiography, where it is assumed that the complete life-story of a person has somehow been captured between the binds. The presumption underlying such a work is that everything about that person has been recollected and laid bare in a book with a beginning, middle and end. The subject's life has been gathered up and *framed*, nothing having escaped the biographer's recall.

As Derrida sees it, all of Western culture is based on books that are believed to contain the truth, the whole truth, and nothing but the truth of our origins. From the Bible through all the great works of the Western literary canon, we see an attempt to capture in full, without any loss of memory, the life-story of our civilisation. The problem is, however, that all texts, no matter how seminal or sacred, do not contain the 'voice' of their authors. As written documents, they are only a partial record of events which have long since faded from memory. While we may frame or bind them between boards in an attempt to contain the original content, it is, according to Derrida, simply impossible to do so. Once something is written down, an element of the original has already been lost or forgotten. That is why, following Kierkegaard, Derrida is less interested in canonical texts than in the 'fragments' which escape from them. He is more interested in what authors leave out than in what they put in, more concerned with what lies on the cutting-room floor than what features in the final edition.

All texts are, in other words, based on exclusion; in editing and cutting, authors exclude things which never show up within the borders of the book. The primary purpose of Derrida's deconstruction is to demonstrate that if Western cultural, political and religious identity is founded on books, and if books are based on exclusion, then Western identity is exclusionary. Its purpose is to show that there is no beginning, middle or end to our story, for beyond the 'secure' borders are fragments which resist incorporation or mastery. Hence he writes an 'autobiography' called *Circumfession* – a title which plays on the words 'circumcision' and 'confession' and which seeks to demonstrate that confession (defined as a comprehensive and accurate account of past events) can never be complete. It is always 'cut' from the origin, severed from the source by virtue of the 'catastrophe of memory'. *Circumfession* takes the form of fifty-nine fragments which appear at the bottom of each page of a biography of Derrida by the philosopher Geoffrey Bennington. It is a dramatic effort to demonstrate that identity, Derrida's included, is disturbed from within by forces and fragments which have been repressed, rejected and excluded from the official narrative.[4]

In the postmodern understanding, culture is, therefore, a construct which must be deconstructed. Borders, frames and structures which rigidly contain their contents, must be loosened up so as to welcome the 'excluded other', the foreign fragment whose arrival cannot be anticipated or controlled. As a form of domestication which establishes and sustains identity, the central texts of tradition must be disrupted and shown to be without firm foundations. They must be read against the grain so as to demonstrate that they are neither seminal nor sacred but simply examples of writing which have assumed canonical status.

However, to do so is to undermine our sense of home. It is to take that which binds, or which provides a common sense of self, and show it to be contrived. Moreover, the consequences of applying deconstructive techniques to university or school curricula are, as I suggested in Chapter 2, that students cease to identify with the great canonical authors, painters or composers, cease to see in their writings and works a pathway to home and self-fulfilment. Rather, by constantly looking between the lines, beyond the borders or outside the frame for the marginalised and suppressed, they are not only alienated from their cultural patrimony. They are also deprived of the timeless moral wisdom which so many of the canonical works in the western tradition convey.[5]

Derrida assumes, because all domestication is a form of mastery, and because culture is domestication, that culture is fundamentally an attempt to control or master what simply cannot be controlled. It is true that culture, in both the everyday and artistic sense of the word, binds people together on the basis of shared symbols, stories, rituals and artworks. However, to conflate this with 'mastery', in the negative sense employed by deconstruction, is to lose sight of culture as a work of love. Of course, it is the nature of culture to retain and conserve, to memorise and memorialise. It does so, however, not in order to exclude but to save and preserve, not in order to suppress but to guard against further erosion of those things we simply cannot afford to lose.

Few people doubt that when things are written down, painted or recorded, they detach from their original source and lose the purity of their creators' intentions. We know that when we read Shakespeare, Dickens or Dante, when we listen to Bach, Mozart or Bruckner, we do not have direct access to those writers and composers. We know there will always be an element of ambiguity regarding their precise intentions when creating their greatest works. However, notwithstanding this so-called 'death of the author', all readers of Shakespeare have a similar experience. While we may differ in our interpretations of *Hamlet* or *Othello*, we know that these plays flowed from the quill of a particular individual who had a unique perception of the human and moral condition. If our perspectives on these plays change, the content of the plays does not. Enough of the spirit or consciousness of the author remains for us to be able to identify the work as belonging to Shakespeare. It is this which gives a work its enduring identity and which enables us to resuscitate it from generation to generation.

To conserve culture means to specify that which is living in what deconstructionists presume to be dead. It is to see in our everyday common culture a source of membership, one not predicated on exclusion but on a common set of values to which all citizens, new and old, may subscribe. It is to live in the light of our forebears, to maintain a sense of their presence by upholding those norms of behaviour, and standards of style, which signify who we are and what we value. A country's culture is the story of how it came to be, how its people chose to adapt the land to their needs and how they sanctified it in word, rite and song. It is the story of how we overcame alienation to establish a settlement worthy of our greatest sacrifice. Without a common culture with which we can identify, without a collective set of customs and stories to which we can subscribe, people will be far less inclined to make sacrifices for their shared homestead. That is because, in the absence of culture, people have little sense of that to which they belong. When culture is written off as something dead, or as something elitist and exclusionary, the social adhesive which binds them simply dissolves.

I do not say that the widespread promotion of fragmentation so obvious in Western thought should be blamed solely on Derrida and deconstruction. That was certainly never Derrida's intention and one that no serious reader of his writings could attribute to him. However, it can be blamed, at least in part, for the pervasive postmodern view that traditional or high culture does not count and that culture's claim to preserve something precious and sacred from extinction is fallacious. In emphasising death and loss over what is living and lasting in culture, deconstruction and all those fashionable postmodern movements which have produced the culture of amnesia have merely succeeded in creating, as Scruton puts it, 'an adolescent community which suffers from an accumulating deficit in the experience of membership'.[6]

The work of conserving culture is difficult and demands constant vigilance. It takes time, effort and dedication to absorb the great works of literature, to come to terms with the great composers and to cultivate the aesthetic sense. It is especially difficult to do so in a society which has become cynically detached from its cultural inheritance. If obviously not the most important, it is one of the reasons why, as stated in the previous chapter, I take my children to the traditional Latin Mass. For there, they not only savour the sacred but connect with their ancestry through word, ritual and song. In emphasising beauty as a revelation of the Divine, and in submerging the ancient rite of the Church in sacred music, this form of the Mass clearly demonstrates why culture matters.

Witnessing this sacred spectacle, you are reminded of what we stand to lose should such 'little platoons' cease to exist. You are reminded why, in the absence of classical languages, children cannot adequately understand their history and, indeed, their language. You realise that the type of music to which we listen defines the type of people we are. Most especially, you understand why, without beauty, we cannot truly belong. For when beauty is replaced by the ugly or banal, people cease to identify with their surrounds. They are estranged and alienated from something which should invite, ennoble and attract. It is then that they experience only absence and emptiness in a place where they should feel most at home, one that should unite them, in as much as it is possible, to the summit and source of their identity. As I shall argue in Chapter 9, there is nothing virtual about this experience. Everything is real, concrete and permanent. People are present to each other, and through the sacred rites, they seek to fuse the present to the past and thus to the future. However, it is an experience which, were it not steeped in the cultural riches of the tradition, would seem far less authentic.

The principal point I want to make is that in a world of virtual and celebrity 'culture', where everything is ephemeral and demands little effort, such experiences offer a striking alternative. For me, the experience of the old Mass is in a realm of its own, in as much as it opens up a resplendent pathway to eternity. However, in the less exalted secular sphere, the concert hall and the art gallery also offer an experience that roots, unites, binds and nourishes. For it is there that people commune with each other through a celebration of their common past and through a shared appreciation of their artistic achievements. This is not a realm of fantasy but one where the imagination is enlivened to a point where it reaches into the very depths of history.

As I say, however, it requires much labour to sustain this experience in a society so dedicated to its disappearance, for this is not something which can be obtained on the cheap. Of course, those in the mode of Hegel's master believe it is possible to bypass the work of culture. They believe that high culture can be purchased at the right price, thereby becoming a personal possession for their use only. However, without the work of culture, in which the self appropriates their meaning, such artefacts will simply become empty icons. Like the master, the celebrity surrounds himself with cultural riches, but he neither understands them nor can he see beyond their superficial qualities. In contrast to Hegel's slave, he is not prepared to invest what it takes to derive true self-satisfaction from his treasure trove. That is why, in the context of such leisure and luxury, they signify vulgarity rather than cultural sophistication.

The guardians of culture, those who sustain the little platoons in the face of indifference, are often derided as cultural 'elitists'. In as much as those people recognise that there is indeed a significant distinction between pop and high culture, and that the latter responds to our human longings much more than the former, the charge of elitism is misplaced. That is because such 'elitists' are not seeking to accumulate cultural wealth for their own private and selfish enjoyment. Rather, their primary motive is to make widely available the most precious and consecrated treasures of our cultural inheritance. If they shun the deconstruction of culture, it is because they recognise that while it is much easier to destroy rather than maintain our 'existing monuments', it is a luxury not worth the cost. For when we cease to care for culture, cease to see it as our way back home, we are left with nothing more than a desiccated ruin. We have nothing which ensures that virtue becomes our habit, nothing that can teach what we ought to value if we are to flourish. We have nothing in and through which we can hear the wisdom of ancestral voices and make it our own.

In placing so much emphasis on culture and aesthetics, Benedict XVI sought to show that their neglect is not something without serious consequence.[7] Neither can be casually dismissed as 'ideology' or as a way of inoculating against critique the particular interests of 'bourgeois' elites. That is because their neglect or loss manifests in widespread social disenchantment and disintegration. As mentioned in Chapter 2, the Pope Emeritus referred to this as a 'dictatorship of relativism', in which nothing is for certain and where people are tossed to and fro by every wind of doctrine. Having dispensed with objective criteria to distinguish between good and bad, beautiful and ugly, the individual becomes his own judge in matters of morality and taste.

It is important to note, however, that while the individual ego is privileged in such a dictatorship, people still yearn for the comfort of culture. They still yearn to belong to something bigger than themselves. As Hegel correctly perceived, human beings naturally desire to surmount the alienation of isolation, instinctually long to be affirmed and recognised by others. However, in a society where high culture has been driven underground, the sense of solidarity it once supplied is no longer available. In response, people satisfy their longing to belong through forms of membership that celebrate rebellion, rejection and homelessness. They unite together on the basis of a shared repudiation of the same or the 'we', in favour of a systematic and uncritical bias towards what is 'different' and 'other'.

As such, pop or postmodern culture takes the form of a collective 'No' to a past from which it seeks to totally disengage – from a past which, as Derrida puts it, has never been present. This 'community without community' is one that revels in that alienation and estrangement, to overcome which was the primary purpose of traditional culture. It is a culture of disobedience whose primary aim is to resist being drawn into the 'circle of the same'.[8] It is a society of strangers that denies inherited identity and refuses integration. That is why the preferred mode of contact in such a 'culture' is *virtual* communication, a form of belonging where people never truly belong, where they remain isolated even when seemingly connected.

If art has a role to play in this postmodern society of strangers, it is, therefore, not to incorporate but to divorce the self from the great eternal society. However, when my children savour music such as Ralph Vaughan Williams' *The Lark Ascending* or Maurice Ravel's *Adagio Assai*, they are liberated from the ego and its desires. They are offered a vision of something higher and nobler than their own interests, something which transforms not only the way they perceive the world but also the way they relate to it and to other people. They have a sense, moreover, that despite having no 'armour against fate', their lives have nevertheless been redeemed from the trite and the trivial. For now they have something against which they can judge the celebrity culture which penetrates so much of their everyday existence. Even at this early age, they can see why Mozart matters more than Miley Cyrus. Simply by savouring the great composers, they can see why it is that those like Schubert offer salvation from selfishness. They also recognise the inexhaustible richness of this music compared to the paucity of pop. In short, this experience of music which once served as the basis of our culture has opened my children's aesthetic sense to the essential poverty of postmodernism. It has taught them to distinguish the genuine from the fake, and how to detect when they are being emotionally and morally compromised by that which sells itself as 'culture' but which, in reality, is a cheap imitation.

That communal experience of music is something familiar to all who still attend the classical concert hall but is denied to the children of Cyberia. For them, music is no longer a social experience but one of total isolation. It is true that they bond with others around their favourite pop performers, but listening to them involves plugging in so as to block the world out. The purpose of the headphone or earplug is to detach from social reality in order to dwell in a reality of one's own. The Cyberian experience of music consists in placing a barrier to social engagement. Where once it was the key to communal harmony, music is now a source of division.

Take, for example, the old song culture which united people at every level of society. This was a culture in which people from all strata could play musical instruments and could draw from a common repertoire of songs. They would gather, share a meal and then sing songs which celebrated their past and idealised their experience of home. Each person would be invited to sing while the rest respectfully listened, joining in only during the chorus. This was no ordinary form of entertainment but one which gave people a sense that they were meant for something more than isolation, that they could rely on others whose experience of the world was no different to theirs.

Wherever people gathered, whether in private homes or in public houses, they would converse and sing. Today, the public house is still filled with music but of a vastly different nature. The booming beat which is now such a familiar feature of the public sphere prevents people not only from singing but also from properly conversing. The result is that even in those contexts which once served to unite neighbours and friends, people remain divided. This contrasts vividly with the way music formerly functioned in the public house. By day, such places were animated by the sound of convivial conversation, and if, at night, there was music, it was not blasted through a speaker but performed by real musicians. This provided the opportunity to listen, sing along or dance. However, dancing in such circumstances was never done alone but with a partner who could move elegantly to the music. In other words, music was not used to separate but to bind people. It was used to overcome distance and division, to forge and foster familiarity. And then, at evening's end, those who had danced away the hours would stand united as the national anthem was played. Having celebrated their common identity through song and dance, it was now time to pay deference to the homestead. The fact that this was also done through a particular song, the words of which everyone knew from an early age, further testified to the pivotal role of music in a society in harmony with itself.

One sign of the extent to which society has fractured is that the national anthem is now rarely played following social events. As I see it, this represents the decline of the experience of music as a powerful force of unity, as that which bound people together in celebration of their common values, community and country. This was not an expression of cultural triumphalism but a tribute to those, both living and dead, whose sacrifices ensured the survival of our settlement. It was a testament to the fact that others surrendered much so that we might have the liberty to sing and dance, to converse and laugh. When people cease to sing their national anthem, it is a clear signal that they have succumbed to the culture of amnesia. When they no longer see fit to sanctify their social gatherings by proudly paying homage to those who established and shaped their settlement, it is an indication that they have radically detached from their origins and lost their sense of self. They no longer know who they are or what they stand for, which is why they stay sitting.

Likewise, we could say that this experience of detachment is promoted by the postmodern architecture that has steadily replaced the 'existing monuments' of old Europe and elsewhere. Traditionally, the purpose of public art and sculpture was to make familiar what would otherwise appear foreign. It was to give personality to a place, to domesticate it so that its inhabitants could recognise it as theirs. Statues took the form of those who best embodied the nation's principles and ideals. In shopping, socialising and strolling among these monuments, people, quite literally, never lost sight of their canonised forefathers.

Walking as a young child through Dublin's main boulevard, I was overawed by the towering figures of stone and bronze which lined the street. These were monuments to people who had fought to secure Irish independence and who, like Daniel O'Connell, had emancipated the country's Catholics from suppression. At every turn, the city spoke of its past and provided a tangible experience of identity to those who dwelled there. Today, Dublin's central boulevard, which is named after O'Connell, is dominated by an enormous icon to nowhere. Standing at a height of 120 metres, and weighing 126 tonnes, The Spire resembles a giant stainless-steel pin. It is a point, as one critic put it, 'without a point', one which directs the eye towards the amorphous ether. Neither a commemoration of past nor a celebration of place, this futuristic icon dwarfs the stately memorials below. Consequently, it is now possible to stroll down that particular street and never notice those, like O'Connell, who beckon us never to forget. The Spire is a perfect monument for a culture that has lost touch with its roots, for a people 'with no direction home'.

If postmodern art is animated by rupture, alienation and dissonance, it is because it is based on a rejection of belonging. Its aim is not to make people feel secure but to shock, unsettle and confuse. Hence there is nothing in the postmodern spectacle with which we can identify, nothing that reminds us of our common heritage and shared space. Indeed, the whole 'point' of something like The Spire is to dislocate, disturb and challenge our sense of space. As a tribute to abstraction, its purpose is to shatter our claims to identity. However, when I gaze upon the statue of Edmund Burke which proudly stands at the front entrance of Trinity College in central Dublin, I have something before me with which I can readily identify.

Erected in 1868, and designed by Dublin-born sculptor John Henry Foley, this statue reminds my countrymen of the fact that this great defender of true liberty was one of their own. It forces us to confront our past as something not solely characterised by narrow nationalism or sectarian bigotry, but as that which owes as much to people like Burke as it does to those like the father of Irish republicanism, and zealous admirer of the Jacobins, Theobald Wolfe Tone. The presence of Burke at the heart of our city reminds us that this man, so often denounced and dismissed by Irish Catholics, did more than most to establish the Catholic National Seminary at Maynooth. As explained by his biographer Russell Kirk, Maynooth 'was meant to elevate the intellects of Irish priests, so helping to save Ireland from Jacobinism'. And, although he 'failed in his attempt to place control of the college entirely in the hands of the Catholic clergy, its establishment with government approval and participation was Burke's final success in his war upon the [anti-Catholic] Penal Laws'.[9]

If postmodern art stands out, it is because it is expressly designed with the intention of not fitting in. It makes a virtue of estrangement and stands in defiance of what is commonly understandable and easily recognisable. In eclipsing the human form, or, indeed, in explicitly emphasising the carnal over the spiritual, it undermines those moral and religious values which animated all art prior to the twentieth century. This is also reflected in the popular sartorial fashions and styles adopted by the children of Cyberia. Having dispensed with established sartorial norms, whereby people dressed elegantly as a symbol of respect for others within the public sphere, the purpose of much contemporary fashion is either to shock, as in those clothes which seek to reveal rather than conceal, or to signify that their wearer has rejected dwelling in favour of detachment.

The ubiquity of casual or leisure wear, and the rejection of formal clothing, signifies much more than a change of taste. It is a rejection of the distinction between the private and the public, one founded on the belief that because the social space belongs of its nature to everyone, we are obliged to behave in it as we would in our own home. Today, however, we live in a society where public–private boundaries barely exist. It seems we no longer know where the private sphere ends and the public begins. This is a world in which people dress only for themselves and where personal comfort matters more than public decorum.

In a dramatic illustration of this, I have even witnessed mother and daughter shopping together in their pyjamas.

If we have sartorial standards, it is because clothes signal our evolution from the cave to civilisation. They represent our triumph over animal life to that of rational beings in search of social and moral perfection. There is, in other words, a great deal of moral wisdom underpinning traditional norms of dress. Clothes polish up the person, thus signalling that he or she values politeness. Dressing well shows that you have made an effort for others. It demonstrates that you consider them worthy of your best. As such, elegance should never be confused with vanity but should be considered as the epitome of grace. It symbolises that we are seeking to fit in rather than stand out.

In the end, culture matters because, whether we accept it or not, and whatever effort is involved in acquiring, conserving and passing it on, it *is* the basis of our common identity. In all its forms, it is that through which we discover who we are and where we belong. It is what gives a people and their place a distinct personality, what binds them to their past and provides the resources for a successful future. That is why the conservation of culture is a moral necessity, for when it is neglected, there is little that can hold the homestead together – little to remind us of our shared heritage and common destiny.

In losing the communal experience of culture, we lose sight of our highest ideals, hopes and longings, all of which are sustained and transmitted through literature, music and art. In dispensing with our everyday cultural customs, we cease to live for one another, opting instead for a life of splendid isolation. When, in other words, we neglect the work of culture, we risk forgetting what it means to belong, what it means to find lasting consolation where estrangement is the only alternative available.

Notes

1   Derrida, *Points…*, p. 387.

2   Derrida, *Points…*, pp. 144–5.

3   Derrida, *Points…*, pp. 144–5.

4   Geoffrey Bennington and Jacques Derrida, *Jacques Derrida* (Chicago: Chicago University Press, 1993).

5   See Chapter 2.

6   Scruton, *Culture Counts* (New York: Encounter Books, 2007), p. 64.

7   See also Chapter 4 of Dooley, *Why Be a Catholic?* entitled 'From Boredom to Beauty'.

8   See Derrida, *Given Time: I. Counterfeit Money*, trans. Peggy Kamuf (Chicago: The University of Chicago Press, 1992).

9   Russell Kirk, *Edmund Burke: A Genius Reconsidered* (Wilmington: Intercollegiate Studies Institute, 1997), p. 199.

9

Saving the sacred

The Latin translation of the word 'religion' is *religare*, meaning to tie or to bind. To be religious means, therefore, to be bound to something greater than the self, something which involves sacrifice, surrender and, in the case of Islam, submission. It is to acknowledge one's complete dependence on the Creator and all His creation. It is to adopt a posture of thanksgiving towards others and the world, one that rejects rights (at least as they have come to be defined) in favour of reverence, responsibility and respect. Religion also involves belonging to a community of believers united together through a shared faith in the sacred source of all things. It is consequently no great surprise that, in our contemporary culture of disobedience, religion has become such an object of suspicion and ridicule. From the high priests of scientism to the prophets of postmodernism, the principal aim is to undermine the sense of the sacred and the form of community which it fosters.

For those like evolutionary scientist Richard Dawkins, religion is nothing but a virulent virus which must be eradicated if human beings are to flourish. Like Nietzsche, who first announced the death of God in 1882, Dawkins believes that we are simply 'clever animals' governed by our genes and that those who believe in God are deluded.[1] For many postmodernists, on the other hand, God is not so much dead as a shadow of His former self. They are not prepared to go the distance with Nietzsche and Dawkins, simply because they consider the declaration of God's death to be yet another absolutist position. To proclaim, in other words, that there is no God is to be no less authoritarian than those who maintain they have definitive proof of His existence. As such, they reject both militant atheism and traditional theism in favour of what John Caputo describes as the 'weakness of God' or 'weak theology'.[2]

Caputo follows Derrida in seeking to give meaning to what both thinkers call 'religion without religion'. This is 'religion' which binds its practitioners to nothing more robust than 'a ghostly quasi-being', to a Messiah that is always to come.[3] Weak theology is one of absence: it rejects the strong 'messianisms' of Judaism, Christianity and Islam, in favour of something which cannot be housed or contained in any temple or tabernacle. On this reading, 'strong theology', the theology of orthodox churches and tenured theologians, endeavours to domesticate or put God in his place. It is the theology of pastors and popes but not that of prophets or the powerless. For the prophet is not one who seeks to make God fully present but one who reminds us that He is still to come.

That is why, according to Caputo, there is no room for true prophets in the Church, an institution which, he believes, has lost sight of its anarchic 'origins'. In proclaiming a kingdom of 'nuisances and nobodies',[4] Christ came not to endorse but to defy the established order. He came not to settle but to unsettle, not to seek out the familiar but to dwell among those who were radically different and other. Strong theology endeavours to obscure its own radical origins so as to emphasise that, in the beginning, 'the Word was made Flesh'. This, according to Derrida, is yet another attempt to conserve what simply cannot be conserved. Recalling my discussion of deconstruction in the previous chapter, it is a refusal to acknowledge that at the core of Christianity is a 'Book', in this case Holy Scripture, which cannot fully reveal the true foundations of the Faith. For, to repeat, all books – even those which are assumed to be divinely inspired – are predicated on exclusion. There is always some degree of loss in the process of trying to preserve the past, or the spoken word, *in writing*. To proclaim, therefore, that the Word has been made Flesh, is to proclaim the impossible. It is to say that God has been made present in that which, of its very nature, is indicative of loss and absence. It is to insist that we can recollect our sacred origins through that which, of its nature, denies us access to them.

According to Caputo, religion without religion 'does not subsume or enclose particulars within or under it, does not precontain them, but simply points an indicative finger at "singularities" that are beyond its ken, kind, genus, and generic appetite'.[5] It affirms what churches and scripture cannot control or subdue – the 'radical other' which they try but fail to forget or deny. It is a religion rooted in faith alone – faith in the 'wholly Other' which can never be made present. This is faith drained of all doctrine and dogma, one that refuses to be bound by the strictures of any particular creed. It is an affirmation of 'God' as absence, an openness to that which cannot be confined within the present order. Hence it is a form of belief directed towards an open-ended future or what Caputo describes as the 'unforeseeable and incalculable'.

If, as Caputo suggests, traditional religion is in the business of excluding and excommunicating, this quasi-religion of pure faith unreservedly welcomes that which is different and deviant. It is unconditionally hospitable to the 'just one who shatters the stable horizons of expectation, transgressing the possible and conceivable, beyond the seeable and foreseeable, and who is therefore not the private property of some chosen people'.[6] Having dispensed with all rites, rituals and sacrifice, it is a 'religion' of mercy which says 'yes' to the outcast, the marginalised, the unknown and the forgotten. If it distinguishes itself from the old 'religions of the Book', it is because they all have the 'makings of a catastrophe, that is, of war'. This they unfailingly provoke, Caputo argues, 'with merciless regularity, under one of the most grotesque and terrifying names we know, that of a "holy war", which means, alas, killing the children of God in the name of God'.[7] Weak theology forms the basis of a religion of resistance to all who would make God their own, to all that proclaim to know what or who God *is* and to those who think they have a divine mandate to do God's bidding here on earth.

It is certainly true that all religions have had a bloody history. It is also the case that they have regularly sought to exclude those who have challenged their creeds. However, if this were the only legacy of the old 'messianisms', they would have few remaining adherents. Take away the sacred sense sustained through the millennia by established religion, and you certainly would not be left with an earthly utopia. Indeed, as the cruel history of the twentieth century so vividly shows, whenever a sacred settlement is swept away by secular ideology, the result is neither peace nor harmony but tyranny, holocaust and enslavement. This is not to say that religion is now immune to fanaticism and fundamentalism. The horrors perpetrated around the globe by radical Islamists clearly demonstrate what can always happen when religion is distorted, when people believe they have a direct line to God. Yet, for the majority of ordinary believers, religion is neither a call to arms nor a blueprint for extremism. It is that which, by uniting them with their sacred lineage, and with absent generations, gives shape, meaning and moral purpose to their lives.

According to its practitioners, weak theology is not in the business of binding or domesticating. It rejects what Derrida calls the 'family scene', in which identity is privileged above difference. That is why it is a theology which emphasises *blindness*, one which affirms what it cannot see and thus what it cannot contain. It seeks to restore 'invisibility to memory',[8] to show that in relation to the origin we are always in the dark. It is, thus, a 'theology' which limits the sense of sight and, consequently, which shields and disconnects believers from the Divine. This is faith in *nothing* – in something so irreconcilably different and 'wholly Other' that it impossible to know what you are meant to be affirming. If, as I believe, this cannot serve as a proper object of faith, it is because faith invites us to unite to something more than 'what is always to come'. As I once asked Caputo in the course of a public debate on this subject, 'What's the point of having a god … if it's [such] a weak force?' He replied by inquiring, 'Would it be possible to think about what's going on "in the name of God" if we could dissociate God from force and power, while retaining the notion of an unconditional claim, something that claims us unconditionally and demands that justice flow like water across the land?'[9] Unless we can *identify* the source of that claim, unless it has a certain *power* to elicit a response, I do not believe it is possible.

Most Christians, for example, are not well versed in theology or even in the basic catechism of their faith. Yet, they live in accordance with Christian principles because they identify with the *person* of Christ. In responding to His claims, they respond to something concrete, to the source of their salvation. In the absence of this personal relationship with the Divine, it is not at all obvious that they would consider the mandate to love unconditionally as anything more than an empty precept. This explains why I define weak theology as a religion of detachment – an opening to something with which you can never reconcile or identify, being as it is so remote and unrecognisable. It is why I think it could never evoke the same passion for justice, mercy or love that established religion has throughout its long history. In the words of Mark C. Taylor, 'sojourners can feel at home only in a world in which the divine itself is at home'.[10] Only when the 'wholly Other' becomes one of us, when it becomes somewhat the same, can it have true force in the lives of believers.

The underlying assumption of weak theology is that traditio-nal religion is predicated on knowledge rather than faith. Having domesticated God, we can now claim *to know* His intentions, *know* with certainty what He wants of us. Faith, on the other hand, does not claim a special relationship with the Divine. With genuine faith, there is always a degree of not knowing and uncertainty. It requires a 'leap' into the unknown, a movement of trust and hope rather than certainty and clarity. Such is the great lesson of Kierkegaard's long meditation on Abraham in *Fear and Trembling*, a dramatic text which seeks to illustrate that 'faith is the highest passion in a person'.[11] In knowledge, all is made abundantly clear and visible. In faith, we can only see through a glass, darkly. However, it is only those on the fiery fringes of religion that claim to have 'absolute knowledge' of God. If ordinary religious believers make no such claims, it is because theirs is a religion which involves a great deal of trust and hope.

Every time believers enter a church, they make an act of faith in that which is unseen. Nevertheless, it is faith in *something* tangible, something to which they can direct their praise and worship. It is to trust that God has entered time and is now really present in their lives. This is not an expression of fundamentalism, not an attempt to contain or subdue the sacred, but simply a humble effort to connect or commune with their Creator. In the case of Christianity in general, and Catholicism in particular, this faith-filled communion does not direct the eyes of the believer elsewhere or, indeed, to nowhere. It is not an attempt to escape the slings and arrows of time and chance. Rather, it is a way of uniting more concretely with creation.

What I want to say is that, in the main, so-called 'strong' religion is neither escapism nor a recipe for fanaticism but a rooted form of faith that inspires love, charity and noble sacrifice. The repudiation of religion is nothing less than the rejection of all those things which serve to connect us to the sacred, the community (both living and dead) and to our common past. For what is religion if not memory, memorialisation and a work of mourning in which the dead are never forgotten? What is it except an offering of thanksgiving for all that we have received and, indeed, for the very fact of existence itself? What is it except an acknowledgement of our dependency on that which is far greater than the solitary self? That is why Burke spoke of the Church as 'the first of our prejudices, not a prejudice destitute of reason, but involving in it profound and extensive wisdom'. It is that which, by rescuing us from the 'paltry pelf of the moment', offers a 'solid, permanent existence'.[12] For through it, we are given a sense that life is rooted in much more that the passing pleasures of secular society.

In seeking to make a home for the sacred, the Church serves as a repository of memory. It endeavours to reconcile believers, not only to their divine origin but to a tradition which memorialises all those who personified the best of Christian virtue. In worshipping at their memorials and shrines, the community invokes the spirit of the saints and attempts to live in their light. It is this which keeps us mindful of their sacrifices, mindful of the fact that without their willingness to preserve and transmit what we now possess, our children would be disinherited from their sacred bequest. In the absence of religion, in the absence of those rites and rituals which connect the living to the dead and the unborn, society loses its memory and fractures at the seams. If this has now become commonplace across the secular world, it is because without religion and the institutions which sustain it, identity loses its underlying cohesion. That is because there is no context in which communities can celebrate or commemorate their common origins, nowhere to give praise for all they possess and nowhere to sanctify their hopes and longings. Where the sense of the sacred is weak or non-existent, so also will be the sense of belonging which all societies require in order to endure.

A church consecrates not only the community but also the land upon which it settles. It serves to bind people to God and to absent generations through acts of faithful adoration. Derrida is correct: in as much as it offers sanctuary to the sacred and the dead, the Church does indeed domesticate. However, it does not seek to 'shut down the very structure of time and history, to close off the structure of hope, desire, expectation, promise, in short of the future'.[13] If anything, it is domestication rooted in the richest form of hospitality or 'openness to the other'. Indeed, at the core of the Catholic religion is the sacred 'Host' – the God Who sacrifices everything for those who come to worship at His table or for those who are made one through Holy *Communion*. In accepting the hospitality of the Host, worshippers are, in turn, commanded to welcome the unborn, the living and the dead. For, that is the true nature of the sacramental experience, an experience that binds us unconditionally to the requirements of others.

In kneeling before the tabernacle, believers are, *in faith*, acknowledging their dependence on the hidden Host and, in turn, vowing to offer hospitality to their dependents and neighbours. The sacramental experience roots them, not only to the source of creation but to creation itself. They are united to the earth, its fruits and to its stewards, both past, present and to come. The seven sacraments of Baptism, Holy Communion, Confirmation, Confession, Matrimony, Holy Orders and the Last Rites provide an experience of the sacred in and through the gifts of creation. Through water, bread, wine, fire and oil, the believer is incorporated into the 'great eternal society' of fellow believers. We are reconciled to God and to one another through eating and drinking, through the consumption and use of substances which feed the body and sustain the spirit. In each case, the purpose is to savour the sacred, to experience God as something real, present and true. Naturally, this demands much faith, but it is something which nonetheless enables us to experience God, not as remote, unrecognisable or indifferent to our needs but as something with which we can tangibly identify. What is more, in uniting with God in this way, we are simultaneously reminded that we belong to a place shaped and moulded in the image of our canonised forefathers. Through the consecration of bread and wine, Christian believers are brought into the 'real presence' of their God. However, they are also reminded, as fellow communicants, that they share a common home, a common past and a joint destiny. For bread is the food of belonging and wine a symbol of our rootedness to time, place and history.

Contrary to Richard Dawkins's assertion that religion is the stuff of fantasy and fairy tales, the sacramental experience convincingly demonstrates that, if anything, *religion roots us to reality*. It sensitises us not only to the requirements of absent generations but to creation and its manifold gifts. It is an experience of the Eternal which does not result in division, detachment or denial but in communion, benediction and belonging. Take away the Church as that which sustains the sacramental experience, and you disconnect from that which unites and binds. You rob religion, not, as Caputo maintains, of its extremist element but of its matchless power to convey an enduring sense of community, identity and settlement.

Of course, this is not to suggest that the question of God's existence is secondary to the social and moral function of ecclesial institutions. The primary role of the Church is to preserve and transmit those theological truths which are the bedrock of the faith. This it does, not in ignorance of the so-called 'catastrophe of memory', for the Church has always been sensitive to the need for theological interpretation. However, as Benedict XVI writes, unless 'there had been something extraordinary in what happened, unless the person and the words of Jesus radically surpassed the hopes and expectations of the time, there is no way to explain why he was crucified or why he made such an impact'.[14] In other words, we can take for granted everything modern exegesis, and indeed deconstruction, tells us 'about literary genres, about authorial intention, and about the fact that the Gospels were written in the context, and speak within the living milieu, of communities', while still believing that 'Jesus really did explode all existing categories and could only be understood in the light of the mystery of God'.[15]

Through its sacred liturgy, the Church seeks to conserve that defining truth. In word, ceremony and song, it recollects and rehearses its founding moments. This ancient rite attempts to transmit to the living that sense of awe and wonder experienced by the first apostles in the presence of Christ. By participating in the ceremony, the community or congregation connects to a living tradition. That it does so through a ritual steeped in culture is because it is through art that we have always attempted to express our sacred longings. It is through painting, sculpture, music and sacred architecture that we have sought to express the inexpressible, to identify with the supreme object of our adoration.

The great tradition of sacred art, which in essence constitutes the Western artistic tradition, can be seen as an attempt to put a face on God, to let His light pierce the fabric of time. Art is that through which the finite mediates with the infinite, that through which we acquire a sense that there is more to this world than mere matter. If Hegel placed art next to religion and philosophy as that through which we acquire full self-recognition, it is because it was, for him, a manifestation of spirit shining through the veil of sense-experience. It is through art in general, and religious art in particular, that we overcome the alienation of finitude. Through it, we are given a presentiment of our eternal home and our sacred settlement. To repeat what I said in Chapter 8 (and as I argued at length in *Why be a Catholic?*), the aesthetic dimension of the liturgy is neither arbitrary nor unnecessary. In the absence of beauty, the experience of the sacred loses its power to attract, harmonise and reconcile.

At its best, religion is homecoming. It enables us to surmount earthly estrangement, but not, as Kierkegaard might say, by escaping to eternity through the back door. Rather, it roots us to where we are, inviting us to see intimations of infinity in the concrete circumstances of everyday existence. The sacramental rites bind us to the great eternal society by rooting us to the world. As I have already suggested, they do so through the symbolic use of material substances such as water, wine, food and fire. In the case of marriage, however, we are, quite literally, invited to put down roots, to build a home for absent generations. We are asked to live sacramentally by sacrificing the ego and its immediate desires, so that the requirements of others might be fulfilled. In this way, the commonplace world is sacramentalised and sanctified.

This is what it means to live in the light of eternity: it is a way of existing that does not seek to contain or control the Divine but one that allows the sacred to shape the manner in which we dwell. It involves responding to the sacred through building, dwelling, settling, cultivating and nurturing. That is why, traditionally, the family paused before and after meals to offer grace. It was their way of giving gratitude, not only for the food before them but also for their settlement, sanctified as it was through countless sacrifices down the generations.

I do not say that *only* religious people care for creation or conserve culture. However, in living sacramentally, you are more likely to do both. That is because religious people ponder the earth, not simply as a playground for their own private possibilities but as a sacred bequest to be sustained for those yet to come. They look at the world as though through stained-glass windows, seeing in it the spirit of absent others and traces of the infinite. The religious are more likely, therefore, to adopt the *pastoral perspective*. They are more likely to conserve and sacrifice for those they cannot see or may never know. They are also more likely to undertake the work of culture which, from their perspective, testifies to humanity's irrepressible urge to connect with the sacred in time. It is this which explains why religious people are natural conservationists and why, despite their putative concern for the environment and for culture, those opposed to religion are not. For when the world and our representations of it are no longer perceived as revelations of truth, beauty or the sacred, they are much easier to squander, misuse and neglect. Take away the sacramental, in other words, and there is little to stand in the way of desecration. As expressed by Benedict XVI, 'the new ideologies have led to a sort of cruelty and contempt for mankind that was hitherto unthinkable, because there was still respect for God's image, whereas without this respect man makes himself absolute and is allowed to do anything – and then really becomes a destroyer'.[16] There are, in other words, zealots and fanatics in every religion – including the new liberal 'orthodoxy', one whose guiding credo is that there is no truth and that man is the measure of all things.

To reiterate, the loss of religion is a loss of home, a loss of all that binds us to the earth, to its sacred source and to each other. To drain religion of that essential experience, to make it one of pure faith without any concrete content, is to trade identity for estrangement. It is to experience the homesickness of Hegel's 'unhappy consciousness', to be a 'stranger on earth, a stranger to the soil and to men alike'.[17] That is why I disagree with Richard Rorty's assertion that religion is what we do 'with our solitude' and with his argument that 'talk about God should be dropped because it impedes the search for human happiness'.[18] It is, of course, true that much religious observance is conducted in private, such as personal prayer and acts of penitence. Still, as I have been suggesting, the root of religion is that it binds the individual to something greater than himself. In so far as it shapes the way he engages with others and the world, religion is essentially *public* and cannot be divorced from its communal context without losing its power to convey theological truth and conserve identity. Neither is it possible simply to drop the name of 'God' as though it were similar to objectionable words like 'outcast' or 'untouchable'.[19] In all contexts and circumstances, those words have caused suffering, exclusion and offence. However, despite the fact that the name of 'God' has often been used to justify violence, oppression and even murder, it has more often been a principal source of comfort, consolation, charity and mercy. Through the saints, martyrs and in the very ordinary but no less noble sacrifices of ordinary believers, we see how this name has unrivalled power to serve the cause of human happiness. Hence, to blame it, or religion, for the atrocities perpetrated in its name is, as Scruton remarks, 'like blaming love for the Trojan War'.

Giving up on God-talk is to fundamentally change the way you relate to reality. It is not just a matter of altering one's vocabulary, or of modifying certain habits of behaviour, but of radically transforming the way *life itself* is experienced and lived. That a person so intellectually sophisticated as Richard Rorty failed to recognise this is perhaps best explained by the fact that he was born into a socialist household and was a lifelong atheist. The truth is, however, that the liberal quest to jettison the word 'God' has not resulted 'in a global civilisation in which love is pretty much the only law'.[20] If anything, the effect has been to divide and distance people from each other, to undermine communities which were once bound together through their common allegiance to the Church. It has resulted in a loss of that spirit of sacrifice upon which absent generations depend, and without which nothing can be conserved. When religion declines, as it now has, people cease to make public professions of faith. They cease to make solemn vows before God and the community that they shall build a home and live lives worthy of both. They cease to factor the unborn and the dead into their actions, plans and projects. In favouring the secular above the sacred, they no longer know what it means to live sacramentally, to dwell at the intersection of time and eternity.

To stand at that intersection is not, as I have been suggesting, a flight from reality. It is to be rooted in a way which radically contrasts with the liberal lifestyle. This is real and tangible communion or communication. It engages and stimulates the mind and the senses, thus enabling us to experience the sacred as something present, lovable and praiseworthy. As such, it radically contrasts with the virtual existence of Cyberia, one that is characterised by ceaseless communication but no real communion. I have suggested that more than any other philosopher, Hegel perceived most clearly the fact that without religion we are destined for unhappiness, for a life of disharmony and alienation. Contrary to Nietzsche and Marx, both of whom believed that religion causes alienation in its adherents, Hegel perceived it not only as a source of reconciliation and redemption but as that which 'unifies social and personal existence and counterbalances centrifugal forces that constantly threaten disintegration'.[21] However, in rejecting the concrete messianisms for the wholly Other – what Derrida calls the *tout autre* – not only 'is the individual set in opposition to the natural and social world, but he also suffers inner fragmentation that alienates him from God'. As such, he is condemned to 'labour under the "infinite sorrow" of separation and loss, and can only "yearn" for the everlasting peace of reconciliation'.[22]

Those, once again, are the words of Mark C. Taylor, an American theologian who first rose to prominence through his writings on Hegel and Kierkegaard in the 1970s. In the decades that followed, he would become a pioneer of theological postmodernism in which God would be 'discredited' and 'disfigured'. Moving from Hegel through Kierkegaard and Derrida to virtual culture, Taylor sought to marry theology and technology, to demonstrate the underlying 'religious' nature of Cyberia. As he wrote in 1999, 'When viewed in the context of the displacement of religion onto art and the eventual transformation of the world into a work of art, which occurs in contemporary media culture, it appears that Las Vegas is, in effect, the realisation of the Kingdom of God on earth. As the real becomes image and the image becomes real, the world becomes a work of art and our condition becomes transparently virtual. In the realised eschatology of the virtual kingdom, nothing lies beyond.'[23] Lately, however, Taylor has come to recognise that dwelling in this virtual kingdom is, in fact, an experience of destitution. He is certainly no conservative, but even this great prophet of postmodernism now believes that the prevailing 'obsession with difference tends to leave us with nothing in common'.[24] Hence, he writes that while 'new information, networking and media technologies have undeniable benefits, they also bring losses that should not be overlooked. It is time, indeed, past time, to slow down and ponder what is slipping away before it is too late.'[25]

In a virtual kingdom where nothing is for certain, where speed is valued for its own sake and nothing is embedded, religion reminds us of what it is that we stand to lose should we refuse to slow down. It binds us to place, time and history, to friends, neighbours and community. The sacramental experience of religion goes well beyond belief, ritual and devotion, however vital and integral they are to the religious way of life. It is, in essence, an experience of *reconciliation* and *atonement*, an experience of being at one with God, of belonging to a place that has been sanctified in His image and to a people whose common destiny you share. It is an experience of home in a world that is homeless.

If liberalism and postmodernism emphasise rupture and amnesia, religion generates a culture of remembrance, responsibility and reparation. For most people, living a religious form of life does not involve excluding the stranger or condemning those of other confessions as infidels or apostates; it does not involve seeing God as someone 'who's going to come in here and slay his enemies and do all the heavy lifting for us'.[26] If anything, it is a way of existence which prioritises hospitality and forgiveness, which makes holy the hours in service and humble solicitude. Far from being an example of theological totalitarianism, this is a work of love motivated and nourished by that sense of mutual dependency sustained and transmitted through religious traditions.

Caputo writes movingly and convincingly of the 'claustrophobic catastrophe' which would occur if there were nothing to 'check the free reign of the "profane", the unbroken rule of the "world", the harsh economy where there are no gifts, where everything has a price'. For the profane is nothing less than 'the degradation of the sacred into acquisitiveness, the truncating of human experience into consumption, leaving us to wander the shopping malls in search of what we desire and relegating us to reality TV to search for what is real'. If the profane life 'is flat and thoughtless', the sacred interrupts the 'closure of secularism ... by means of the event which stirs within the name of God'. Secularism means the 'rule of the world, the regime of the profane'. It attempts to 'disenchant the world in virtue of which everything we mean by God is reduced to the economy of the *saeculum,* where everything has a market price'.[27] Hence, if theology is to counter the profane, it must re-sacralise 'the settled secular order, disturbing and disordering the disenchanted "world"'.

There is nothing in that with which I disagree. However, I am not convinced that the re-sacralisation of the secular order, of this our profane paradise, can happen in the absence of the concrete confessions which terrify weak theology. After all, at a time when the large majority of people have long since ceased to read theology, it is unlikely that its effects will again be felt beyond clerical circles or outside the narrow confines of the university. When, however, the sacred has a home, when it dwells among us in a form to which people can relate and with which they can easily identify, it is possible to resist the regime of the profane. Even now, when people are so disconnected, there is a still an immense hunger for identity and belonging. There is widespread desperation for that sense of rootedness which I have sought to defend throughout this book. We see this in the way they seek to connect through sport and through social media sites like Facebook and Twitter. That, however, is an ephemeral form of identity which cannot satisfy beyond the moment, and certainly can never fulfil our deepest yearnings.

The presence of the churches in the midst of the profane kingdom offers a powerful experience of home to the destitute and dispossessed. They offer a concrete alternative to a culture of amnesia and alienation. They demonstrate what it means to live the virtues of faith, hope and love in a society that no longer believes in them. They provide a safe sanctuary from secularism and a sense of belonging to those estranged from everything and everyone. They offer redemption, consolation and reconciliation with the earth and its inhabitants. Without the churches, and without the example of those who dedicate their lives to them, there could be little resistance to profanation. So long as they prevail, therefore, the closure of secularism will not be complete. So long as they, and the people shaped by them, continue to give witness, the rule of the world will be unsettled by the sacred. That is why the work of saving the sacred is not a matter of undermining religious institutions but of conserving and caring for them.

Naturally, I recognise that, in Europe at least, the churches are almost empty. I recognise that the old rites of passage, sanctified and conserved by religion, are in decline and that the sacred has almost vanished from the public square. To many, it seems that the regime of profanation has finally triumphed and that where signs of the sacred survive, they too must be banished. Still, those who celebrate this seeming victory of the profane over the sacred ought to be mindful that *all* societies, including liberal ones, depend on sacrifice, commitment and devotion for their survival. It is doubtful, in other words, that where the churches have finally shut their doors, the habit of sacrifice will continue to shape people's lives. It is doubtful that they will be bound by anything more than virtual relations or that they will be attached to anything greater than the passing fancies of the present age. This is why countering the 'pathologies of religion' by destroying any claim that it has on us is to risk social and moral decay. In short, when the churches decline, so too does everything they actively conserve and transmit by way of sacred ceremony, moral teaching and theological truth which takes concrete form in a life of faith. All of which leads me to conclude that if the Church is 'the first of our prejudices', it is because without it, the work of conservation does not stand a chance. And if that is so, then, sadly, neither do we.

Notes

1   See Richard Dawkins, *The God Delusion* (New York: Mariner Books, 2008).

2   The phrase 'weak theology' is a play on Italian philosopher Gianni Vattimo's expression 'weak thought'. See Vattimo, *Belief* (Cambridge: Polity Press, 1999), pp. 34–5.

3   John D. Caputo, *The Weakness of God: A Theology of the Event* (Bloomington: Indiana University Press, 2006), p. 9.

4   This phrase belongs to John Dominic Crossan. See his *Jesus: A Revolutionary Biography* (San Francisco: Harper, 1995), p. 54.

5   Caputo, *Deconstruction in a Nutshell*, p. 177.

6   Caputo, *Deconstruction in a Nutshell*, p. 164.

7   Caputo, *Deconstruction in a Nutshell*, p. 161.

8   Derrida, *Memoirs of the Blind: The Self-Portrait and Other Ruins*, trans. Pascale-Anne Brault and Michael Naas (Chicago: The University of Chicago Press, 1993), p. 47.

9   'From Radical Hermeneutics to the Weakness of God: John D. Caputo in Dialogue with Mark Dooley', in Marko Zlomislić and Neal DeRoo (eds), *Cross and Khôra: Deconstruction and Christianity in the Work of John D. Caputo* (Eugene: Pickwick Publications, 2010), pp. 327–47.

10 Mark C. Taylor, *Journeys to Selfhood: Hegel and Kierkegaard* (New York: Fordham, 2000), p. 122.

11 Kierkegaard, *Fear and Trembling*, trans. Howard and Edna Hong (Princeton: Princeton University Press, 1983), p. 122.

12   Burke, *Reflections*, p. 78.

13   Caputo, *Deconstruction in a Nutshell*, p. 163.

14   Benedict XVI, *Jesus of Nazareth* (London: Bloomsbury, 2007), p. xxii.

15   Benedict XVI, *Jesus of Nazareth*, pp. xxii–xxiii.

16   Benedict XVI, *Light of the World: A Conversation with Peter Seewald* (San Francisco: Ignatius Press, 2010), p. 54.

17   Hegel, 'The Spirit of Christianity and its Fate', in Richard Kroner (ed.), *On Christianity: Early Theological Writings*, trans. T. M. Knox (Gloucester, MA: Peter Smith, 1970), p. 186.

18   Rorty, *Philosophy as Cultural Politics*, p. 4.

19   Rorty, *Philosophy as Cultural Politics*, p. 3 and Mark Dooley, 'The Plagues of Desecration: Roger Scruton and Richard Rorty on Life After Religion', in Fran O'Rourke (ed.), *Human Destinies: Philosophical Essays in Memory of Gerald Hanratty* (Indiana: University of Notre Dame Press, 2013), pp. 312–36.

20   Richard Rorty, 'Anticlericalism and Atheism', in Santiago Zabala (ed.), *The Future of Religion* (New York: Columbia University Press, 2005), p. 40.

21   Taylor, *Journeys to Selfhood*, p. 35.

22   Taylor, *Journeys to Selfhood*, p. 41.

23   Mark C. Taylor, *About Religion: Economies of Faith in Virtual Culture* (Chicago: The University of Chicago Press, 1999), p. 5.

24   Taylor, *About Religion*, p. 2.

25   Mark C. Taylor, *Recovering Place: Reflections on Stone Hill* (Columbia: Columbia University Press, 2014), p. 2.

26   Caputo, 'From Radical Hermeneutics to the Weakness of God', p. 331.

27   Caputo, *The Weakness of God*, p. 290.

Conclusion

Homecoming

As I have defined it in this work, conservatism is not a refusal to face reality. It is not a wistful yearning for a time long since gone. If anything, the work of conservation reattaches us to reality, to the world, its people and its sacred source. It is the work of overcoming alienation and estrangement, of disconnecting from Cyberia and learning again how to live as we humans should. Hegel rightly believed that all identity involves recognition. To find self-fulfilment, we require the affirmation, acknowledgement and endorsement of others. We require that the earth be recognisable as ours, that it reflects our longing to belong. If we are to feel at home in this world, we must be able to identify with it, to see it animated by the 'spirit' of the living and the dead. The unhappiness of the present age stems from the fact that people are starved of recognition and identity. Having detached from the earth, and their history, culture and religion, they are inwardly destitute. Like Hegel's master, they want for nothing, and yet nothing is all they have. The illusion of self-mastery is predicated on a denial of dependency. However, the fact remains that we are dependent creatures, beings that cannot truly flourish in the absence of family, friends and absent others.

My aim here was not to make a case for ideological conservatism, but simply to suggest that we cannot experience true contentment or self-satisfaction without the work of conservation. This, to repeat, does not mean returning to some halcyon pre-postmodern period. Rather, it requires only that we cultivate that sentiment which, 'in the relationships of our daily life and under ordinary conditions, habitually recognises that the community is one's substantive groundwork and end'. It requires that, in seeking the solace of selfhood, we affirm our dependency on others and the world around us. It demands reigniting the lamp of memory so that we may rediscover the true comfort of place, culture and the sacred. As such, this is a philosophy of affirmation and hope – not the groundless utopian hope of liberalism but hope in a concrete future rooted in the wisdom of the past.

The labour of reattachment is not something that requires a grandiose plan or scheme. It is a simply a process of preserving and passing on, what Burke called, 'the ruling principles of our forefathers'. It is to live, not for ourselves alone but in constant awareness of absent generations. It is to cultivate the habit of sacrifice in our daily life so that, in turn, others may reap a due harvest. This we do by adopting the pastoral perspective in all our domestic dealings. By factoring the earth into our everyday decision-making, and by teaching children how to unite with the soil, we come to recognise just how essential creation is to human identity. We simply cannot feel at home without sensing that we belong to the earth and that it, to some extent, also belongs to us.

Homebuilding, homecoming and homemaking all require endowing a particular place with personality. Through culture and ceremony, we make a house a home. Simply by breaking bread together, people affirm their shared hopes and common belonging. In listening to good music, reading great literature and in attaching children to their cultural inheritance, isolation gives way to a sense that we belong to something lasting. We bind ourselves to that which is ours and which enables us to rehearse, on a daily basis, the success of settlement. Conserving culture is a work of love, for it allows the young to connect with their dead and thus to grow up 'in an atmosphere of example and general custom'. It is that through which the life of the so-called 'individual' 'widens out from one little world to other higher worlds', apprehending 'through successive stations the whole in which he lives, and in which he has lived'.

If religion is vital to this experience, it is because it keeps us forever mindful of the earth, of our responsibility to it and to others. It keeps us mindful of our cultural patrimony and of our debt to the dead. In uniting us with the sacred, it unites us with all creation. In the midst of our 'communications' culture, it stands as a towering testament to the value of true *communion*. In a world so dedicated to the pursuit of individualism and isolation, it is obvious that religion will diminish and decline. However, without the communal endorsement it supplies, and without its power to reconcile people to their sacred origins, it is equally obvious that society will find it difficult to withstand trauma and threat. As Hegel correctly perceived, we cannot feel truly at home on this earth without the binding power of religion. Unless the finite can identify with the infinite, we are destined for disharmony and division. That is why, in ceasing to believe, we very often cease to belong. I do not say that people must return to religion in order to undertake the work of conservation. However, I think it is equally true to say that unless we can preserve the world that religion made, and unless we can foster a sense of the sacred in all our daily dealings, we will lose something precious and vital. We may, of course, survive, but it will be survival only in the most specious sense.

There are, in sum, many roads home. We are not condemned to perpetual isolation, to a life devoid of love, attachment and belonging. At any time, we can unplug from the virtual kingdom and return to reality. We can cease to live a life of opposition and rejection, opting instead for one of affirmation – affirmation of all those things which liberals denounce as our manacles, but which, in truth, are the foundations of true happiness and real freedom. If this requires work and effort, it is not without the consolation of knowing that we now dwell where our roots are strong and where the things that matter are rarely, if ever, forgotten.

Bibliography

Hannah Arendt, *The Human Condition* (Chicago: The University of Chicago Press, 1974).

Aristotle, *Nicomachean Ethics*, trans. J. A. K. Thompson (London: Penguin Books, 1976).

Benedict XVI, *Jesus of Nazareth* (London: Bloomsbury, 2007).

Benedict XVI, *Light of the World: A Conversation with Peter Seewald* (San Francisco: Ignatius Press, 2010).

Geoffrey Bennington and Jacques Derrida, *Jacques Derrida* (Chicago: Chicago University Press, 1993).

Edmund Burke, *Reflections on the Revolution in France* (New Haven: Yale University Press, 2003).

John D. Caputo, *Deconstruction in a Nutshell* (New York: Fordham, 1997).

John D. Caputo, *The Weakness of God: A Theology of the Event* (Bloomington: Indiana University Press, 2006).

David E. Cooper, *A Philosophy of Gardens* (Oxford: Oxford University Press, 2006).

John Dominic Crossan, *Jesus: A Revolutionary Biography* (San Francisco: Harper, 1995).

Richard Dawkins, *The God Delusion* (New York: Mariner Books, 2008).

Jacques Derrida, *Of Grammatology*, trans. Gayatri Chakravorty Spivak (Baltimore: The Johns Hopkins University Press, 1976).

Jacques Derrida, *Given Time: I. Counterfeit Money*, trans. Peggy Kamuf (Chicago: The University of Chicago Press, 1992).

Jacques Derrida, *Memoirs of the Blind: The Self-Portrait and Other Ruins*, trans. Pascale-Anne Brault and Michael Naas (Chicago: The University of Chicago Press, 1993).

Jacques Derrida, *Points...*, trans. Peggy Kamuf and Others (Stanford: Stanford University Press, 1995).

John Dewey, *The Later Works 1925-1953*, vol. 12, ed. Jo Ann Boydston (Carbondale: Southern Illinois University Press, 1987).

Mark Dooley, *The Politics of Exodus: Søren Kierkegaard's Ethics of Responsibility* (New York: Fordham, 2001).

Mark Dooley, *Roger Scruton: The Philosopher on Dover Beach* (London: Bloomsbury-Continuum, 2009).

Mark Dooley, *Why Be a Catholic?* (London: Bloomsbury-Continuum, 2011).

Mark Dooley, 'The Plagues of Desecration: Roger Scruton and Richard Rorty on Life After Religion', in Fran O'Rourke (ed.), *Human Destinies: Philosophical Essays in Memory of Gerald Hanratty* (Indiana: University of Notre Dame Press, 2013).

Mark Dooley (ed.), *A Passion for The Impossible: John D. Caputo in Focus* (New York: SUNY Press, 2003).

Mark Dooley, *The Roger Scruton Reader* (London: Bloomsbury-Continuum, 2009 and 2011).

Mark Dooley and Liam Kavanagh, *The Philosophy of Derrida* (London: Acumen, 2007).

Mark Dooley and Richard Kearney (eds), *Questioning Ethics: Contemporary Debates in Philosophy* (London: Routledge, 1999).

Hubert L. Dreyfus, *What Computers Still Can't Do* (Cambridge: The MIT Press, 1992).

Hubert L. Dreyfus, *On the Internet* (London: Routledge, 2001).

T. S. Eliot, 'Tradition and the Individual Talent', in *The Sacred Wood: Essays on Poetry and Criticism* (New York: Alfred A. Knopf, 1921).

Michel Foucault, *The Order of Things* (London: Routledge, 1970).

Michel Foucault, 'The Subject and Power', in Hubert L. Dreyfus and Paul Rabinow (eds), *Michel Foucault: Beyond Structuralism and Hermeneutics* (Chicago: Chicago University Press, 1982).

Mary Ann Glendon, *Rights Talk: The Impoverishment of Political Discourse* (New York: The Free Press, 1991).

G. W. F. Hegel, *Philosophy of Right*, trans. T. M. Knox (London: Oxford University Press, 1967).

G. W. F. Hegel, 'The Spirit of Christianity and its Fate', in Richard Kroner (ed.), *On Christianity: Early Theological Writings*, trans. T. M. Knox (Gloucester, MA: Peter Smith, 1970).

G. W. F. Hegel, *Phenomenology of Spirit*, trans. A. V. Miller (London: Oxford, 1977).

Martin Heidegger, 'Building Dwelling Thinking', in Martin Heidegger (ed.), *Poetry, Language, Thought*, trans. Albert Hofstadter (New York: Harper & Row, 1971).

Leon Kass, *The Hungry Soul: Eating and the Perfecting of Our Nature* (Chicago: The University of Chicago Press, 1994).

Richard Kearney, *Poetics of Modernity: Toward a Hermeneutic Imagination* (New Jersey: Humanities Press, 1995).

Søren Kierkegaard, *Two Ages: The Age of Revolution and the Present Age: A Literary Review*, trans. Howard V. Hong and Edna H. Hong (Princeton: Princeton University Press, 1978).

Søren Kierkegaard, *Fear and Trembling*, trans. Howard V. Hong and Edna H. Hong (Princeton: Princeton University Press, 1983).

Søren Kierkegaard, *Either/Or vol. II*, trans. Howard V. Hong and Edna H. Hong (Princeton: Princeton University Press, 1990).

Søren Kierkegaard, *Works of Love*, trans. Howard V. Hong and Edna H. Hong (Princeton: Princeton University Press, 1995).

Russell Kirk, *Edmund Burke: A Genius Reconsidered* (Wilmington: Intercollegiate Studies Institute, 1997).

R. D. Laing, *Politics of the Family* (Toronto: CBC, 1969).

Alasdair Macintyre, *Dependent Rational Animals: Why Human Beings Need the Virtues* (Chicago: Open Court, 1999).

John Stuart Mill, *Of Liberty* collected in Mill, *Utilitarianism* (London: Fontana Press, 1962).

Kenneth Minogue, *Alien Powers: The Pure Theory of Ideology* (London: Weidenfeld & Nicolson, 1985).

Józef Niznik and John T. Sanders (eds), *Debating the State of Philosophy* (Westport: Praeger, 1996).

Michael Oakeshott, 'On Being Conservative', in Roger Scruton (ed.), *Conservative Texts* (London: Macmillan, 1991).

Paul Ricoeur, 'The Creativity of Language', in Richard Kearney (ed.), *Dialogues with Contemporary Continental Thinkers* (Manchester: Manchester University Press, 1984).

Paul Ricoeur, *Time and Narrative, Volume 3* (Chicago: The University of Chicago Press, 1988).

Paul Ricoeur, 'Life in Quest of Narrative', in David Wood (ed.), *On Paul Ricoeur: Narrative and Interpretation* (London: Routledge, 1991).

Paul Ricoeur, 'Memory and Forgetting', in Richard Kearney and Mark Dooley (eds), *Questioning Ethics: Contemporary Debates in Philosophy* (London: Routledge, 1999).

Richard Rorty, *Contingency, Irony, and Solidarity* (Cambridge: Cambridge University Press, 1989).

Richard Rorty, *Philosophy and Social Hope* (London: Penguin Books, 1999).

Richard Rorty, 'Anticlericalism and Atheism', in Santiago Zabala (ed.), *The Future of Religion* (New York: Columbia University Press, 2005).

Richard Rorty, *Philosophy as Cultural Politics* (Cambridge: Cambridge University Press, 2007).

Richard Rorty and Pascal Engel, *What's the Use of Truth?* (New York: Columbia University Press, 2007).

Jean-Jacques Rousseau, *Emile* (New York: E. P. Dutton, 1968).

Jean-Jacques Rousseau, *The Social* Contract (Harmondsworth: Penguin, 1972).

John Ruskin, *The Lamp of Memory* (London: Penguin, 2008).

Michael Sandel (ed.), *Liberalism and its Critics* (New York: New York University Press, 1987).

Roger Scruton, *The Classical Vernacular: Architectural Principles in an Age of Nihilism* (Manchester: Carcanet, 1994).

Roger Scruton, *Philosophy: Principles and Problems* (London: Continuum, 1996).

Roger Scruton, *Animal Rights and Wrongs* (London: Continuum, 2000).

Roger Scruton, *Modern Culture* (London: Continuum, 2000).

Roger Scruton, *The West and the Rest* (London: Continuum, 2003).

Roger Scruton, *A Political Philosophy* (London: Continuum, 2006).

Roger Scruton, *Dictionary of Political Thought* (Hampshire: Palgrave Macmillan, 2007).

Roger Scruton, *Culture Counts* (New York: Encounter Books, 2007).

Roger Scruton, *Beauty* (Oxford: Oxford University Press, 2009).

Roger Scruton, *Green Philosophy* (London: Atlantic Books, 2012).

Mark C. Taylor, *Disfiguring: Art, Architecture, Religion* (Chicago: University of Chicago Press, 1992).

Mark C. Taylor, *About Religion: Economies of Faith in Virtual Culture* (Chicago: The University of Chicago Press, 1999).

Mark C. Taylor, *Journeys to Selfhood: Hegel and Kierkegaard* (New York: Fordham, 2000).

Mark C. Taylor, *Recovering Place: Reflections on Stone Hill* (Columbia: Columbia University Press, 2014).

Gianni Vattimo, *Belief* (Cambridge: Polity Press, 1999).

Marko Zlomislić and Neal DeRoo (eds), *Cross and Khôra: Deconstruction and Christianity in the Work of John D. Caputo* (Eugene: Pickwick Publications, 2010).

Index

www.ingramcontent.com/pod-product-compliance
Lightning Source LLC
Chambersburg PA
CBHW050211270326
41914CB00003BA/365